SCENES FROM THE PAST

BOLTON

ENGINEMAN

.............A LAST LOOK BACK

It is the 17th July 1965 and in **Eric Bentley's** superb portrayal of the Down side at Bolton's Trinity Street station, a special rail motor awaits passengers from their holiday at Paignton. It is a fair bet that the vast majority of those joining the little train will be employees from Horwich Works and the holders of privilege tickets. By the time this picture was taken, only one of these competent 2-6-2 tank engines remained in active service at Bolton. In June of 1965, 84017 wandered off to Stockport to join 84013/4/26 which had been there from December 1964. The only other example of this type, and the first of the class to be allocated to Bolton, 84019, was in store. Bank Hall's Class 4MT, 4-6-0 75047, waits patiently with its train ready to form the 17/37 stopping train to Liverpool Exchange. Over the top of the platform canopy, and roughly above the 4-6-0's dome is a small building rather like a sentry box. For those signal men hardy enough, this was the toilet at the Down box. I wonder what health and safety would say about that nowadays?

JIM MARKLAND

COPYRIGHT © JIM MARKLAND 2004

ISBN 1 870119 78 9

ALL RIGHTS RESERVED

DESIGNED BY FOXLINE (PUBLICATIONS) LIMITED

PRINTED BY THE AMADEUS PRESS LIMITED,
    CLECKHEATON, W.YORKSHIRE

PUBLISHED BY FOXLINE (PUBLICATIONS) LIMITED
P O BOX 84, BEDBURY. SK6 3YD

CONTENTS

**THIS BOOK IS
DEDICATED TO**

REBECCA

'Ozzie'(Oswin) Leigh was one of those unlucky chaps who took thirty nine years to be booked a driver. On some occasions when, as a passed fireman, and not required for driving, he could, and did, fire for drivers only 3 or 4 years older than himself. Many of these 1919 men were surplus to requirements and were sent on loan to places far afield on the LMS system. Postings to such as Rugby and Carlisle were not uncommon. The ploy used by the railway company at that time was to create discontent in the hope that these men would eventually become so 'cheesed-off' with continually moving that they would leave the service. Ozzie was one of a number of drivers trained to deputise when the regular Running Shift Foreman was not available. Here, in that capacity, with the chimney of the gas house standing out boldly between two Stanier machines, Ozzie relays a message to the driver of one of them. Ozzies favourite saying of anyone feeling the cold was, *'If theyr't cowd tha wants t'change thi butcher'*. The date in this portrayal is Friday July 21st 1966.
E F Bentley

The author amidst some of his collection of railwayana in his dining room/museum at St Annes on the Sea.

Blackpool Evening Gazette

THE 'BOLTON ENGINEMAN' A LAST LOOK BACK

Taking a further look back on the railways days of steam I have attempted, in this third volume, to widen the picture to include grades other than locomen. The stories or anecdotes portray a way of life that is vastly different from a computerised twenty-first century. The Engine - mens Arrangements books were all hand written. A day would start at 12.01am and would finish at 11/59pm. A dot after the hour would signify 'am' whilst a forward slash referred to 'pm'. Two books would be written up concurrently for alternate weeks; therefore, two books provided a continuous chronological record.

When men were needed to sign on urgently, staff was dispatched, often in the small hours to "knock them up". Frequently, passed cleaners were given this onerous task. I have a very vivid memory of being on such a mission, having at my disposal my pushbike. The man needed was in bed. Standing on the pedals of my cycle, and he leaning out of the window the note was delivered. During hours of darkness my bicycle torch was a great asset, many streets were ill lit by quaint gas lamps. The light they emitted was barely adequate. Even the internal telephone system used by British Railways to connect the Motive Power Depot with "Control" and all the various departments such as signal boxes, shunter's cabins and the guard's signing on point at Orlando Bridge had its origins in LMS days. Each place had its own code. Bolton MPD was short-long - short. Orlando Bridge was long-short-long, whilst Burnden Junction signal box was three short. A time check was provided on a daily basis. In Bolton's case by whoever operated the telephones at Trinity Street station. At the appropriate time, - on the stroke of 9.00am, an operator, or perhaps operators operated every circuit bell and buzzer to every point many times. That signified it was 9.00am! Clocks were set by it.

Steam and railways always had a special place in my mind from early days. Whilst still only a toddler my parents took me to the railway yard at Astley Bridge sidings. There, I could peep through the fencing to see the wagons. During the nineteen fifties my father worked at Harwood Vale Bleaching Company. As a foreman warp sizer he had a small steam engine at his disposal. It drove the machinery in the dry croft. Whilst on my six weeks school holiday I looked forward to taking his dinner to work at 12/00 noon, trespassing on the fields of Dewhurst Farm in order to take a short cut. The factory fairly oozed intrigue when the machinery was in operation. There was, too, the smell of steam and freshly dried cotton after the bleaching and sizing processes had been carried out. Another pull in the direction of steam engines. Then of course there was that first expedition into "train spotting". It took place during the summer of 1951/2 on a footbridge, which spanned the Bolton to Blackburn line just south of The Oaks railway station. In my minds eye, I can still picture Black Five No. 45216 of Bank Hall shed, as she approached, bogie tyres gleaming, working hard up the 1:72 as she lifted the 9.45am, ex London Euston up the bank on its way to Colne. There were other trips out spotting, but not too many. The footbridge, which formerly spanned Bolton station yard and which linked Trinity Street with Great Moor Street, was a haven for those of us carrying ABCs. Lever Street footbridge near to Bolton East Junction signal box was the other main venue where we could hear the block instrument bells ringing in the 'box describing each train. On the opposite side of the footbridge we could see one of Bolton's little saddle tanks on Rose Hill pilot about its business shunting at 'B' side goods yard. *... continued on page 4*

The enginemen's arrangement books were arranged to cover a fortnight's work. Whilst one was in use, the next one would written up. This page is from 1961.

Courtesy Steve Leyland

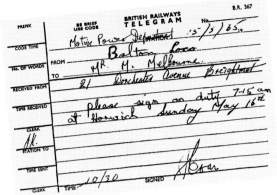

(Above) Not many locomen had the convenience of a telephone in their homes. Instead, when men were required to sign on at a different time or needed to work a rest day "nocker ups" were dispatched armed with notes similar to the ones illustrated.

During 1954/5 this would be either 51486, 51511, or 51513. At Bolton, the highlight of the afternoon would be the passage of a Glasgow to Manchester train. Occasionally, unusual Jubilees might turn up. I have recollections of waiting to see 45696 *Arethusa* of Carlisle Kingmoor, at Weston Street bridge and of No. 45672 *Anson* of Camden shed whilst on the bridge over the station yard at Trinity Street. Whilst around the same period 45695 *Minotaur*, a Farnley Junction engine was noted. These then were just about the limits of my 'spotting' activities. Starting work at Bolton's Crescent Road Motive Power Depot in January of 1956 as a fifteen year old, came as a shock to the system after life at school. The conditions under which we worked as engine cleaners were little short of appalling. Freezing cold in the winter, equally cold cleaning oil and filthy sponge cloths with which we were expected to get the grime off. The fitters too often fared little better. Stripping down an ejector or an injector was a greasy, dirty job. At the other end of the spectrum one had to grapple with hot fixtures and fittings, some of which, such as fire bars, baffle plates or steam valves were heavy and awkward to handle. Life at a running steam shed was far from a bed of roses. There was though, often, that sense of 'excited anticipation', especially when, as a passed cleaner you were next in line for a firing turn. A fireman might fail to turn up, or some train or another might require relief. Often, disappointment was encountered. In 1956 as I began my footplate career things looked bright with the entire main classes more or less complete. But those who had been around a few years longer than I saw a bleak future ahead, for the diesels were just around the corner. Jumping on ahead to 1967, and the final twelve months or so of steam operation, there were one or two consolations. Three or four locos had been afforded attention at factory in 1965/6. Returning from either Cowlairs or Crewe works these had been

The telephone system was, to put it mildly somewhat antiquated yet it did function very well indeed.

'mothballed' until the time came to bring them out of their slumbers to replace those units for which there was no serviceable future. At about the same time, traffic levels were declining and the sidings that we knew so well were closing. By 1968, we had modern, easy to handle forms of motive power. But where was the traffic it was going to move? Much of it had by then taken itself off the railway and on to our roads. So it was that in November of 1968 I also took my leave of railway work and later became a salesman. My heart though lay, and still lies in the power that saw this country through the Industrial Revolution ....Steam!

Jim Markland   St Annes on Sea

(Above) The buildings on our smallholding are a bit neglected as we look eastward around 1955. Harwood Meadows was home to me from 1945 until 1974. The land on which our dog 'Chummy' is seated is now covered with housing. *Author*

(Below) Looking in a westerly direction from behind my Harwood home was this view. Winter Hill dominates the scene un-adorned, as yet by the television mast, which was to follow. From the left we can see the cooling tower of Halliwell power station, more to the foreground, nestling on the hillside above our Harwood Meadows chimney pots is the roof of Crompton cinema. A little further to the right in the centre is Harwood Vale Bleach works. Sadly, all trace of this friendly little factory have now gone. *J M Bentley*

(Top) Astley Bridge sidings just as I remember them. Ex L&Y saddle tank No. **51408** poses for the camera during 1961. During November of the same year this little 0-6-0 moved to Agecroft from where it worked for a further three months up to withdrawal in February of 1962. *C M A Townley*

(Centre) Out of service at Agecroft shed during March of 1962. 51408 looks in a sorry state. A far cry from her days on number 1 pilot where I had many a firing turn aboard the 0-6-0. *R Picton*

(Below) Our 'spotting' activities were divided between Bolton Trinity Street footbridge and, as shown here, Lever Street footbridge near to Bolton East Junction. In this 1968 view, **4472** *Flying Scotsman* passes under the bridge on its way through Bolton. *Authors collection*

The 11.30am Brindle Heath to Bolton has come over the fork line and propelled its train into "B" Side where it is now making up a train, which will form the 1/00pm to Royton Junction. On April 21st 1960, when this scene was captured, it was quite a reasonable days work for an "Austin Seven". At this time the class was in great decline. **49637** lasted until June of 1961 and was cut up at Horwich in October of the same year.　　*D Hampson*

At "B" Side, motor fitted 2-6-2 tank No. **84013** pauses whilst shunting its train brought from Moses Gate where it had acted as pilot on May 2nd 1960. When not required on the Horwich Rail Motor these BR class 2MT tanks were often employed on shunting turns at Halliwell, Bullfield, Moses Gate or here at Rose Hill. The man in the left mid background is carrying water. 'B' Side did not, at that time, have a mains water supply connected.　　*D Hampson*

One of my most prized 'cops' whilst train spotting in 1955 was that of Jubilee 4-6-0 No **45695** *Minotaur*. I vividly remember seeing her after the abortive visit to Crescent Road shed in that year as she thundered over Weston Street bridge. Here, the 5X is leaving Blackpool Central in fine fettle with the 7/15pm to Leeds City South on July 22nd 1963. *Frank Dean*

There were no short cuts to engine cleaning. To do the job properly, everything needed specific attention. In carrying out this duty lots of the grease and grime transferred itself to one's overalls. When cleaned with an oil based cleaner, and provided the paint-work was reasonably good the effect was satisfying. At Blackpool Central shed, Jubilee class 6P 4-6-0 No 45580, *Burma* gets spruced up on May 26th 1961. *Frank Dean*

(Right) Bolton was lucky to have a supply of volunteer engine cleaners. Many of our locos at Bolton were kept spick and span by them. Here, Paul Salveson, nearest the camera and Keith Pendlebury devote their attention to Stanier 8F No.**48652** sometime during the latter half of 1965. *Authors collection*

(Centre) Another scene from late 1965. More of the volunteer cleaners are working on Black Five No.**45318**. at Bolton shed. From the left they are: Steve Leyland, Martin Leyland and Vernon Sidlow. *Paul Salveson*

(Below) As part of our training to become cleaners "passed to act as firemen" (passed cleaners), the Motive Power Instruction Car paid a visit to Bolton shed during October of 1956. As well as the car along with its working models of locomotive valve gear and a locomotive faceplate, the footplate inspector came to deliver a series of lectures. All these were held in a small room, which was once the canteen. Special emphasis was placed on Rule 55, the protection of trains. This scene is from 1949. In the foreground with barely concealed cigarette is driver George Merry secretary of the Mutual Improvement Class (MIC) Immediately behind George partially concealed is fireman Bill Martin. The man in the smock coat is Inspector Cudworth. *courtesy Bert Welsby*

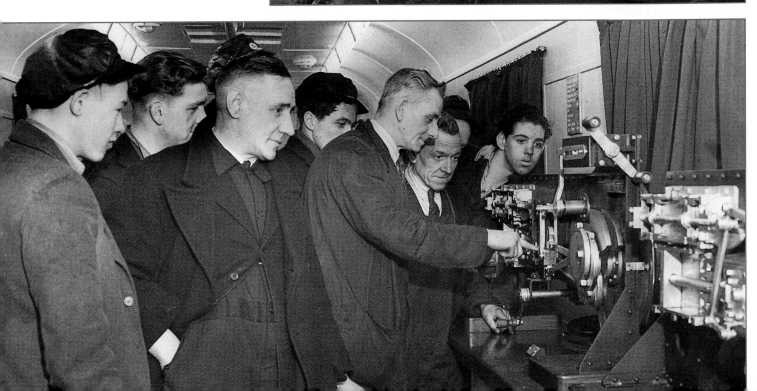

The first Black Five to arrive at Bolton in February of 1962 was **45290**. In this portrayal at her home depot on March 28th 1965, she is not long off the shops, having been back at Bolton shed only a matter of three weeks since her visit to factory. One of a few locos a treat to work on toward the end of steam. This Black Five's number plate has survived as a part of my collection of railwayana.   *H L Holland*

Stanier class 8F No. **48773** makes a grand sight as she operates an enthusiast's rail tour past where Bury Gas Siding formerly stood. The special was the last steam operated passenger train on this particular branch. A visit to Crewe works during May of 1966 ensured that 48773 would be 'in' on the end of steam.   *Ray Farrell*

(Right) Stanier Black Five No. **45110** was in a very rough state when she arrived from Stafford on July 18th 1965. It was only to be expected that an early shopping proposal would be submitted. By April 22nd 1966, the 4-6-0 had reached Cowlairs works and was away from Bolton MPD for a total of fourteen weeks. The loco actually arrived back at Bolton at 10/40pm on 22nd of July, having left Cowlairs works a week earlier. 45110 became famous as she was used in the 'end of steam' specials. ***M S Stokes***

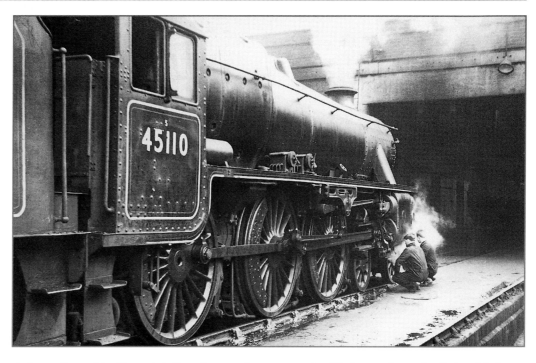

(Below) Returning from Crewe works on the 10th October 1966, **73069** was probably the last Bolton engine to receive repairs. Much work had been carried out even down to supplying a newly cast smokebox number plate. Surprisingly, 73069 had also been reboiled along with considerable work to the valve gear. I never remember it being run down after that, and it always strikes me as a great pity that the preservation movement had not, at that time, become well established. Having found a new home at Carnforth after the closure of Bolton to steam the BR Standard 4-6-0 operates a ballast train at Carnforth on July 17th 1968. ***Frank Dean***

By May of 1958 I had become the owner of a brand new Ariel 350cc Red Hunter motorcycle very similar to this 500cc Ariel Huntmaster.
Authors collection

(Right) Life at a running shed was often dirty, and was always smokey. When locos were lit up from cold there was nothing to disperse the smoke, which just hung in the lower atmosphere. The Stanier machine outnumbers a lone WD Austerity 2-8-0 on April 16th 1967. *H L Holland*

Just about everything concerned with footplate work was dirty, heavy or hot, - or all three! To say that I'm speaking about the time when steam was the main source of power on the railways is I hope obvious. You could though make life on the footplate as bearable as possible. For years I carried my own handbrush to sweep up with on board and carried around a BR type gauge lamp until the day came when it accidentally got left behind on a footplate. I'd had it painted in the same colours as the 350cc Ariel Red Hunter motorbike I'd bought during May of 1958. That super machine had set me back £230.15.9d and was my pride and joy of the day. Whether a driver, fireman or passed cleaner, if you were preparing an engine, or worse still, several engines, Monday was always the worst day of the week to do it. Those very early turns, from midnight onwards were horrid. At Bolton, some engines not required over the weekend until the following Monday would have their fires withdrawn on Friday. Most of the others not needed until Monday would have had their fires thrown out on Saturday. By the time Sunday morning came round when, on the 8.00am shift, the steam-raiser re-lit them, many were cold and without steam in their

boilers. After the firebox had been coaled round, lighting-up was often crudely achieved using oil soaked sponge cloths, the firelighter stocks having been exhausted. For the next two or so hours, because there was no steam pressure to help the smoke away up the chimney it would find the easiest way out, via the fire-hole doors. It caused a real mess in the cab. Large lumps of soot which we nicknamed "blackjacks" formed all over the faceplate and the inside of the cab roof. It was a mess! The lighting in the shed yard was never adequate, and before the advent of the Bardic battery operated lamps, the only other light a driver had was a small torch lamp. Resembling a mini watering can, and with a one inch wick made from worsted trimmings they were fuelled and filled via a screwed on brass cap with rape oil. The same stuff that we used in the gauge lamps, it was obtained from a large blue bottle made from tin-sheet metal on the counter in front of the stores on number one road. The smoke these little lamps gave off had to be seen to be believed. When using them underneath a locomotive in order to see the oiling points on a Bissell truck or bogie they would crackle and spit when droplets of water fell among their flames. For drivers,

the operation of physically going underneath an engine standing over a pit presented a major hazard. He might just have forgotten to tell his fireman that he was going beneath the cab. Without thinking, the fireman might then start to swill down in the cab. In a matter of seconds the driver would emerge dripping with black water from the coal dust. Some drivers would pull out the wicks much too far. One chap who mis-treated them so would remark,*"Tha wants t' be able t' see wi' um mon"*. Even the crews signing on for a passenger working, often between 2.00 and 3.00am had engines to prepare other than their own. With all these goings on, the clean overalls you'd come to work in were soon dirty if you didn't watch out, and in those days, Monday was always washing day for the ones worn during the previous week. On the footplate something had to be done about all that soot, otherwise it soon ended up on one's face. Putting the hose straight on to it was of no value; it simply blew the soot all over the place, but mostly on us. The routine was firstly to turn off both boiler water gauge glasses in order to ensure that when we finally used the hose, water of a different temperature coming into contact with them didn't cause them to burst. Next, fill

Smoke and grime were part and parcel of the steam scene. This view taken from the top of the coal hopper in 1961 illustrates the point very well. On number one road, **40063**, one of the long stored Fowler 2-6-2 tanks, has been pressed into service. On number 2 road stands one of the Stanier class 3MT tanks No. **40137** of 9A Longsight shed. *Author*

an oil can with oil and from its spout, pour the contents all over the faceplate and let it dribble right down. For the next few minutes, the best thing to do was fill the headlamps and boiler water gauge lamp by which time the oil would be ready for swilling off with the hose pipe. If you were careful, you could avoid wetting the drivers and fireman's seats by tipping them up. Finally, it was always a good idea to retire to the mess room to make a brew whilst things on the footplate dried up. Once off the shed and backed up to our passenger stock, perhaps whilst the steam heaters were warming up the carriages in the siding, I would set about cleaning up the brass fittings, and the gauge glass protectors so I could actually see boiler water levels. For the next few hours, the footplate would be my working environment so some time was spent in a general clean up of footplate fixtures and fittings. But back to preparation duties, oiling up the motion-work was always the driver's job. At Bolton, there were formerly two sheds, one of which (Plodder Lane) was on the LNW side. By the time I had started my footplate career in January of 1956, the other Bolton station, Great Moor Street, had closed. The LNW shed at Plodder Lane too had succumbed along with that closure. However, there

survived a little freight work and some LNW men signed on duty at Crook Street goods yard for a time after the closure of their depot. A number of men from Plodder Lane transferred to our L&Y Crescent Road depot. Some L&Y men resented their presence. Occasionally, dirty tricks were resorted to. A favorite prank was to bang in the corks on an engine's motionwork when it was known that an LNW man would be the next to have to oil it. There was too, open hostility when rival factions were paired together. So far as L&Y drivers were concerned, LNW firemen could tell them 'nowt' about 'A' classes. Whilst it is widely known that when an LNW 'Super D' was entrusted to an L&Y driver his heart sank into his boots. The fear was real. On one occasion, as a passed cleaner, I was marked for firing on Halliwell to Healey Mills, empty coal wagons bound for the

Yorkshire coalfields. There was nothing hard about the turn for which, at that time we signed on around 8.25am, the turn number was 307F. That day, we started from Kearsley, and the job was made hard by the driver because we were given 49400, one of the LNW 0-8-0s. The driver became really bad tempered, finding fault with everything and only spoke once to me during the whole journey, telling me to leave the blower valve alone. We had an uneventful trip down the Calder Valley line and were relieved, as usual at Hall Royd Junction, just beyond Todmorden. The return working was a heavy coal train with a mucky Austerity at the front of Crofton to Edge Hill, a train carrying locomotive coal to that latter depot. The transformation in the fellow was amazing. Sat on the 2-8-0, waiting a road, we discussed everything from BBC Television's 'Grandstand' to gardening, all the tension was gone once we stepped off the 7F. To round off the oiling side of preparation duties, there were a number of chaps who often said much of the oil, especially that poured into the connecting rod small end simply ran away as the engine moved and it was therefore a waste. These were the chaps who kept their overalls clean from Monday to Saturday; they always seemed to know that the chap before them had given it a good oiling. Or did they, perhaps just leave it to chance? They were well known, but were in the minority. I bet they scored full marks with their wives though when washing day came along!

Smoke and grime. Taken from a ladder up one of the lighting towers at Bolton shed very near to the end of steam. *Bart van der Leeuw*

Men from the "Lanky" were seldom at home on the LNWR "Super Ds". The fear of something different from what they were accustomed to was a real one. The fact of the matter is that these 0-8-0s were useful machines and could pull enormous loads, but in Bolton mens' eyes they were foreigners. Crewe North Black Five No. **45257** receives rear end assistance from **49447**, a Springs Branch loco after leaving Bamfurlong on a Coventry to Heysham spoil train on Saturday November 18th 1961. *E F Bentley*

In unusually clean condition, Austerity 2-8-0 No. **90143** is at the head of a rake of empty hopper wagons similar to those we would be operating up the Calder Valley line loaded up with slabs of best Yorkshire coal bound for Edge Hill MPD. The 8F pictured on the Through line, is about to attack the route via the Loop line and Cheetham Hill out of Manchester Victoria on May 7th 1960. *Frank Dean*

CHAPTER TWO

THE MEN WHO DROVE THE TRAINS

Generally speaking, the drivers with whom I worked at Bolton's Crescent Road Motive Power Department were decent souls. Some of them however were a mystery. I often ponder, even today, over thirty years after leaving footplate work, just how some of them had gained their knowledge. Many of the ideas which they perpetrated were downright stupid, whilst some of their methods made one wonder where they had been all their railway life. One driver swore that a certain cure for a stiff regulator gland was to pour a measure of oil into the water tank. His idea was that some of the lubricant then found its way to the stiff gland. He never could understand why others had never thought of the idea! The same fellow who, incidentally was thought, (quite wrongly) to have been a good engineman also had his own ideas about 'warming up' the cylinders. At Bolton, we had an early morning job, which took us light engine to Horwich station to work a passenger train to Manchester. His 'idea' was to run the whole of the six miles light to Horwich with the cylinder cocks open. Then, once coupled up to the three coaches, perhaps whilst steam heating the train, he would leave the taps shut, to keep the heat in!!! The mind fairly boggles doesn't it? All the way to Horwich with the cylinder drain cocks open, and therefore, the atomizers not working you can hear the engine groaning. Then, of course they would be stood coupled to their stock for perhaps twenty minutes or more. The cylinder cocks now closed, the steam atomizers were working. The steam from the atomizers would condense. When departure time came you can almost hear the water squelching out of the piston glands-and from anywhere else it might escape. What the fitting staff would say about all the foregoing doesn't leave much to the imagination. The same chap was often of an awkward and unpredictable nature. He persistently interfered with his fireman's work and on many occasions drove him to despair. Three or four weeks was the norm for one man to stay as his regular mate before asking for a move. On one occa-

Bolton's 2-6-4 tank No. 42626 is coupled to the motor set almost ready to operate the last passenger train out of Horwich during September of 1965. It is probably standing in a similar position to that train where the driver with his 'theory' of running all of the six miles to Horwich with the taps open stood with his train. *H Scowcroft*

sion, a strapping fireman was so upset he took the fellow by the throat and would have belted him only for the fact that the driver spat out his false teeth in the encounter. The episode ended with the pair of them on hands and knees by the side of the track until the mucky molars were recovered and washed in the bucket on the footplate. When time permitted, the same driver couldn't resist wandering about stations to see what was going on. With a few minutes to spare at Manchester Victoria station in Oldham bay platforms he took a stroll. The fireman was busy on the footplate. When departure time arrived there was no driver to be found and a relief had to be summoned. With the delayed train now departed, the driver was eventually found trapped in a goods lift, which had stuck between floors. Because of the resultant delay, paper was flying about in all directions until an explanation was delivered. The driver had no business in the lift but somehow, he got away with it. Along the perimeter of Bolton shed yard a fence made of sleepers marked the

boundary with Back Crescent Road. During the hours of darkness, the same chap would have a look through the sleepers to watch the antics of courting couples. To do this, the smallish man had to get well down beneath a gas pipe, which was secured to the sleepers about eighteen inches or so from the ground. One night, whilst so engaged, a much taller chap came along to look over the fence. Standing on the gas pipe to see better he almost choked the living daylights out of the smaller man. A much talked about subject during my footplate days was 'jimmies'. Some drivers had their own made to measure items and carried them around just in case they got on a steam shy engine. Some, as a matter of course would fit the device when they got an 0-6-0 of the 'Derby Four' variety, just to be sure of a good trip. 'Jimmies' were fitted to the orifice of the blastpipe. Often they were fashioned from a metal bucket handle. The ends of the handle were then firmly wedged on the inside of the blastpipe and positioned centrally. With the device now

Although Horwich was something of a bleak outpost standing as it did at the foot of Rivington Pike, you always felt at home there. It was as if life was a pace or two slower. Here, the motor is in the siding ready to dash out and quickly propel its train back into Horwich's single platform to operate the 4/57pm to Blackrod once the 4/54 to Bolton has departed. *N R Knight*

in place, when the engine was working, the blast was effectively cut in half so that it was made to fill the chimney more. This in turn caused more air to be drawn in via the fire bed causing the fire to be hotter with the result that the engine steamed more freely. Of course, there was a price to pay. The engine burned much more coal under those circumstances. It was however, often said that when the device was removed the engine steamed much worse than before it was fitted. This was due to the carbon on the inside of the blastpipe having become pitted resulting in an uneven blast. In one extreme case, a driver regularly on the bank engine had a 'jimmie' hidden in the tunnel at Bradshawgate. When an "A" class was on the banker he would fit his very crude device, which consisted of a metal bar placed across the blastpipe top and held in place by a set of wagon links, which were then allowed to dangle down the side of the blastpipe. Because of the excessive combustion produced it was impossible to push more than three or four vehicles. You can fairly imagine the noise, the spark throwing and the fireman bending his back shovelling the coal into that white-hot firebox. In the end, one fireman got so fed up with it all that he went in search of the hidden 'jimmie'. On finding it he dragged it from its hiding place in the tunnel and lobbed it, unceremoniously into

the canal beneath the viaduct a little further up the bank. That was the end of it. 'Wire drawing' was a subject, which caused a lot of spark throwing. It was one I often wondered about so far as the name was concerned. A story often told to me by one of my drivers was of his days firing on the Aspinall 2-4-2 Radial tanks whilst on passenger work. Occasionally, one of his drivers, who said he knew of the art of 'wire drawing' and locos in general indulged in this practice. With the regulator well open and sparks flying off the

chimney top the fireman asked just what he was up to. "I'm wire drawing," came the reply." Good heavens, I thought you were fire drawing", said the fireman. Wire drawing is a term relating to the procedure of making wire. Molten metal is pulled, or drawn through a hole in a hardened steel die. As the process develops, so the metal is 'drawn' through holes of smaller and smaller diameter until the desired thickness is attained. The process was analogous to steam passing through the main steam pipe and being 'pushed' through a

During the earlier years of my employment at Bolton shed, and right up until 1962, Bolton boasted an allocation of 'A' classes. These 0-6-0's of Aspinalls design going right back to 1889 were the 'maids of all work' on the L&Y. Various 3F's made Bolton their home as did **52123** an arrival from Nottingham, on January 10th 1953 until it departed for Southport on July 9th 1955. The date of this scene on Bolton shed is February 1953. *M J Blackburn*

It looks like 52461 has just been lit up on Sunday May 27th 1956 on number one road at Bolton shed. In all probability the loco would be diagrammed to work the 7.22 trip from Bolton East to Bullfield the day following. This particular loco was one of ten engines of this class said to have been built as a result of an economy drive by the collecting together of spare parts. The engines were built during 1917/18 and the clue to their identity is the narrow angle valance beneath the footplating. The locomotive behind is a Stanier 2-6-2 tank running in after overhaul at Horwich and will no doubt operate the station pilot at Bolton on the day following. It was commonplace to stable these engines on number one road over a weekend. Both crews signed on at 5.45am and each crew had their own engine to prepare. *Authors collection*

narrow opening of a partly closed regulator valve. Steam pressure would be reduced but its velocity would be speeded up. At the valves the speed of the steam would be reduced again. Because the valves were continuously opening, all it meant was that the engine was operating at less than boiler pressure. The idea that most chaps knew about this and what they were doing is highly suspect. In fact, on the old L&Y and its machines, most drivers pulled up the wheel a couple of turns or so. Then, once up to speed, they pulled the regulator back towards the closed position until the engine was running satisfactorily. This then was 'wire drawing'. Just how many knew exactly what they were doing is a matter for conjecture. Not all the drivers were like that of course. For a time, Bolton had on its books a number of the LMS Compounds. I just missed out on that era. Unfortunately, Bolton did not have the kind of work best suited to these machines and their six foot nine inch driving wheels. Instead, much of Bolton's passenger work consisted of stopping trains. Therefore, the Compound principle was not, at Bolton, exploited to it's fullest.

Many of Bolton's passenger turns were

stopping trains to the port of Liverpool and return to Rochdale. All in all, more than thirty stops and starts. One fireman had been on such a working with a driver who had worked "simple" engines rather than in full compound. On the return journey, having climbed Westhoughton bank, and reaching the level bit before Chew Moor, the driver slipped the regulator over into compound. *'Nay'*, said the fireman, *'lets finish off 't job as wiv bin aw day an' run simple engine'*. On the other side of the coin, Johnnie Tickle, who was only about five feet five inches tall, was great in stature when it came to operating these machines as they were meant to be handled. After four or five 'puffs' up the chimney, over would go the regulator into full compound working. From that point onwards, the working of the engine, and the steam used was governed by use of the reverser. The fireman had a play day. This was artistry indeed. Staying with an L&Y theme, and in particular the Aspinall 2-4-2 tank engines, another story in this chapter also relates to the line from Wigan to Bolton. One damp and very misty winter's evening, dusk was just falling as one of these machines was climbing the bank from Hindley to Westhoughton.

Entering the cutting, with four coaches on the drawbar, serious slipping became a problem. With the slipping, the fire became beaten up, white-hot. The engine started to blow off, just as they slipped themselves to a standstill. The driver, a man of a very short fuse indeed, flew into a rage. His idea was that they had come to a stand because of the blowing off. Stepping across the footplate, he grasped the fireman's jacket lapels and buffeted him repeatedly against the cab side sheeting. Obviously, the fireman was not going to take it lying down and he hit the driver hard, once only. Then, taking the controls, the fireman skillfully re-started the train and told the driver to fire, if he could. That was how the day finished, with rolls reversed. The two never spoke to each other again! Three weeks later, a move up for the fireman took him on to goods work and well away from that driver. Those sorts of chaps were in the minority; they were the exception rather than the rule. Most of the men were cheerful souls; many wanted to make the job as easy as possible. Occasionally, drivers, especially those younger passed firemen who were of an 'easy going' disposition might be taken advantage of by some firemen of perhaps a rather stronger personality. For a number of years we had a freight turn on a Saturday evening which took us first of all as passenger to Todmorden. From that point we were booked to relieve a working going back to Bolton. On one occasion, the footplate crew travelled as prescribed and made their way to the locomens relief cabin close by where the Copy Pit bank engine waited. The fireman was a very forceful character and somewhat self-opinionated. At the other end of the spectrum, the driver was a thoughtful pipe smoking individual and somewhat inclined to a quieter disposition. A card game was in progress and the fireman soon joined in. The driver partook of his supper and followed it up with a pipeful of 'bacca'. Time passed on very pleasantly indeed. After a while, because he was nearer the telephone, the driver suggested that the fireman make some enquiries via control as to where their train was as it was now very late. The response the driver got was a rude remark. Nothing was done. More time went by after which the driver decided to phone control himself.

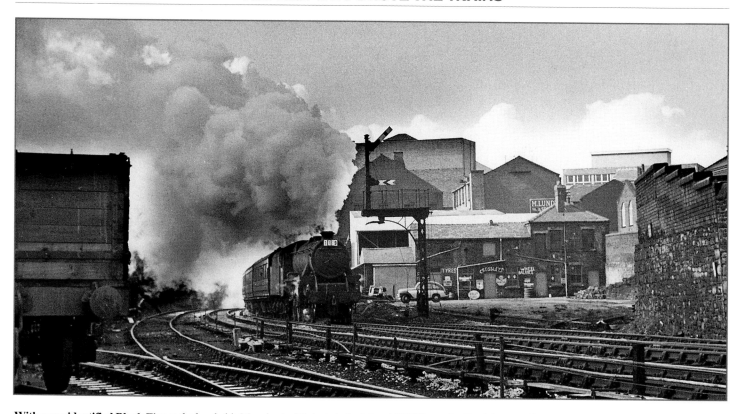

With an unidentified Black Five at the head, this Manchester Victoria to Ingleton ADEX is passing Bradshawgate just outside Bolton on the line to Blackburn. To the right of the 4-6-0 is the short siding where the bank engine waited . The small 'dummy' or 'dolly' signal enabled access to the main line when a banker was required. The yard right background was formerly a small coal yard. During the mid nineteen fifties it was Bullfield pilots last job around midnight to deliver loaded coal wagons there using a little 0-6-0 saddle tank of L&Y origin. The date here is April 12th 1963, Good Friday!   *E F Bentley*

The official told him that the turn had been cancelled. Instructions had been passed to L&Y control in Manchester. The message had never been passed to Bolton shed! Arrangements to get back to Bolton now had to be made. The last passenger train over the Pennines had long since gone. A ride in a brake van was arranged over Copy Pit line with them walking part of the way to Blackburn where they caught the first passenger train back to Bolton. The fireman was held not to have been responsible and was paid in full. The driver however was only paid for a flat eight hours and was on the receiving end of a 'Form One' reprimand. During the middle part of the evening we had a turn where we were booked to walk to Bolton to relieve a working to Hellifield. The driver spotted a freight passing toward Bolton quite slowly. *'Hey'*, he shouted, *'hop on to the running board and we'll get a lift at least part of the way'*. Quickly, things started to happen with the distant for Bolton East clearing and the train picking up speed. *'Jump off quick'*, shouted the driver. By now though speed had picked up and signal wires and points

and crossings intervened. *'Not likely'*, called the fireman. *'What are we goin'ter do then'?* said Jim. *'I know what I'm going to do'*, called the fireman. *'I'm going to make myself comfy on board till this train stops'*. The guard hearing the talking came on to the verandah of the brake van and told them it was a part fitted - next stop Blackpool. Luckily, they were able to screw the hand brake on hard enough in order to slow the train down so they could jump off on the Through road at Bolton. Thus, they were let off the hook and were able to carry out their booked work. I often wonder what some of the old hand drivers would make of our modern-day car boot sales. Drivers rate of pay was never 'over the top', so like most Lancashire folk they liked a bargain. Entering the driver's lobby one afternoon I was surprised to see one of the 'old hands', Joe Eccles, of Kearsley Pilot link wearing a pair of tatty old spectacles. One of the earpieces was missing. The chap was though finding the glasses suited his state of vision perfectly. *'Good grief Joe'*, I remarked. *'Where the heck did yer get them things from'?* *'Why'*, he says,

'they're fine, afe a creyn o 'Farnerth Market, dead mons glasses'. It was well known that occasionally things went home from work which really ought not to have done. Sponge cloths after they had been washed made ideal floor cleaning cloths and some of the issue of Swarfega, which we had at our disposal, went missing. One afternoon a discussion was taking place on the subject of pilfering. The drivers lobby was fairly crowded. One man, previously silent whilst making out his ticket, now joined in, saying he had never stolen a single thing from the railway. From over the other side of the lobby came the rejoinder, *'no but think of all them times yer were late on duty but still booked on at reet time Bill'*. *'Ah, well'*, came the reply. By the time I had entered the footplate fraternity the writing was on the wall for steam. British Railways 1955 modernization plan was well under way. Soon, some steam sheds would have strange bedfellows. The diesels were coming! After the Second World War, food was often in short supply. One driver whom I will simply call Roger...............*continued on page 19*

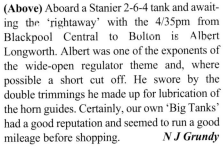

(Above) Aboard a Stanier 2-6-4 tank and awaiting the 'rightaway' with the 4/35pm from Blackpool Central to Bolton is Albert Longworth. Albert was one of the exponents of the wide-open regulator theme and, where possible a short cut off. He swore by the double trimmings he made up for lubrication of the horn guides. Certainly, our own 'Big Tanks' had a good reputation and seemed to run a good mileage before shopping. *N J Grundy*

(Top-right) Albert Longworth again in typical pose, hand on driver's brake valve and keeping a sharp lookout ahead aboard a 'twenty sixies' tank. *N J Grundy*

(Centre-right) Hughes 'Motor' No. **10606** at Blackrod on the Horwich pull and push train. The 0-4-0 was at Bolton from June 5th 1937 until withdrawal took place on November 20th 1943. The date therefore is somewhere in that slot. Not much difference in the ages of the fireman, Jim Widdowson on the footplate and driver Bill Croston. ***Authors collection***

(Lower-right) From the early nineteen fifties comes this relaxed scene of railwaymen on their annual social club outing. On these occasions any rivalries there might have been twixt the LNWR Plodder Lane shed and the L&Ys Crescent Road depot were put aside in favour of a good day out. The location is not known but the subjects are from the left Storeman Dick Davies (Plodder Lane); Driver Norman Bamber (Crescent Road); Drivers Ernie Rothwell and Bill Brown (Crescent Road); Driver Joe Glover (Plodder Lane); Driver Bill (Ginger) Lees (Crescent Road) and lastly, a very young looking Tommy Jordan, Passed Fireman (Crescent Road). *courtesy G Glover*

(Above-left) Seen here on the right, driver Joe Axford will always have a special place in my memory. For many years because of a chronic ailment, Joe was confined to shed duties and disposal work. On one occasion during the early part of 1956, Joe was working the 7.30am disposal turn. I had managed to evade the watchful eye of the foreman cleaner and sneaked off to help shed 'Austin' 49532 off the bank shunt. After helping to turn the engine by hand on the turntable, (the Austins had no vacuum equipment) Joe allowed me to drive the 7F into the sheds. At only fifteen years of age it was a big adventure. Sadly, Joe never made it to retirement, for during 1963, his chest complaint got the better of him. Bert Welsby, shortly to become MIC secretary, is on Joe's right. The backdrop is Stanier 2-6-4 tank No. **42657**. The year is around 1951. *courtesy Bert Welsby*

(Above-right) One of Bolton's 'balanced' Stanier Class 8Fs has arrived at Horwich with a trip from Bolton. The train is ready to set back on to the loco works. In the cab of the 2-8-0 on the right is Fireman Alan Brooks whilst on his right Driver Jack Ashcroft leans on the gangway doors. Date of this happy scene is August 18th 1965. *courtesy A.Brooks*

continued from page 17..............always seemed to know someone who could supply whatever was required. Often, contacts were met in the pub. He had a very large appetite and one of his favourite dishes was a kipper. When he took them to work he fried them on the shovel. When cooking was complete he tore off the heads and tails, wedged them into buttered barm cakes and devoured the lot, bones and all with great relish. He had though, one alarming disposition. He often stepped into the road without looking to see if there was anything approaching. When told about this he would simply say, *'they've got brakes, let 'em use em'*. Eventually, the inevitable happened. On leaving the pub after a heavy session drinking he walked into the road straight into the path of an oncoming car. That was the end of him. Nicknames were a speciality of footplatemen. They loved to make them up. One elderly driver had become dubbed 'Sitting Bull'. On boarding the footplate of the elderly 0-6-0 saddle tanks on "B" side pilot he sat himself down on the sandbox lid, which

also doubled as a seat. Next, his smelly pipe was firmly clamped twixt his teeth. His movements were very ecomomical. The only time that effort was needed was when he moved his mouth in order to grumble. The ground staff were heartily sick of him and were glad when he retired. Some of the older drivers were perfect gentlemen. I got a pleasant surprise when one of them, Harry Mellor, invited me to drive. Admittedly we were only on Horwich Works pilot, but to a seventeen year old as I then was, it was an honour, especially when you remember that Harry was at that time sixty-four years of age. When steam relinquished control of shunting operations at Bolton's Rose Hill, or 'B' side as it was locally known, a number of the older hand drivers were trained to drive the English Electric 0-6-0s. Suitable names were soon thought up for the chaps and their new charges. Bill Spargo's favourite talking point was the dipstick, - so 'Dip-stick Bill' he became. Harry Holmes suffered a failure of the unit, and as a result was nicknamed 'Flat Battery Harry'. For some reason,

Teddy Worrall was known as 'Lectric Ted' whilst Jack Rawlinson was dubbed 'Oil fuel Jack'. Just how Jimmy Bennett became known as 'Monkey Bennett' I'm not quite sure though the shape of the eyes etc might have had some bearing on it. Tommy Brown was always referred to as 'Pal' Brown; maybe he used it instead of his fireman's name. A very important role was played by firemen who were passed to act as drivers. They were known at Bolton as 'spare men'. More officially they were 'passed firemen'. Often they arrived at work to sign on duty for firing. At short notice they were promoted to the status of driver, sometimes on to 'special' work. On many occasions, they could be sent to relieve a turn running behind schedule. This would often be work not normally covered by Bolton depot. On one such occasion, during the early part of 1958, a 'passed fireman' who had booked on at 8.54am to relieve the middle turn of Kearsley Pilot with an elderly driver was so promoted. At about 9.00am, the telephone attendant handed him a slip of paper with the words, *'Special, Heaton*

Mersey - Hellifield, 48323 relieve at Manchester Vic'. A 'passed' cleaner at that time, I was given the job of firing. We were told to get to Bolton and board the first train we could to Manchester. The 'special' was waiting. The crew would go no further, and the train was blocking the through route. Hurriedly, we walked up the track to Bolton station just in time to board the 9.17am departure. This train had left Colne at 8.00am and conveyed through carriages for London Euston. From Bolton, the train was first stop Manchester Victoria, then on to Stockport where two through coaches were attached to a train from Manchester's London Road station. No sooner had we boarded the train, which consisted of eight side corridor coaches than off it went. In the front coach we found two empty seats, one on each side of the compartment. Very smartly dressed men and women occupied the other seats. Most of them looked down their noses at us. I had been engine cleaning earlier that day and my overalls were somewhat greasy. Over my shoulder was slung haversack with food and brew can in it. On my head, the usual locomans greasetop hat adorned with the standard issue BRITISH RAILWAYS badge. My youngish driver however was somewhat tidier. Instead of a serge jacket he wore a rather good 'bomber' jacket and a matching fawn coloured, soft flat cap. By the

time the express was passing Bolton shed in about a mile, speed was nicely built up to about fifty miles an hour. This also heralded the arrival of a very official looking ticket collector. Looking at Wilf, my mate, he demanded to know for what purpose we were travelling. The piece of paper with train details was waved at him. Regrettably, the paper didn't even have British Railways on it. The man took a dim view of the situation and from the outset adopted a firm stance. Playing to the audience, his view was that my mate wasn't even dressed in railway clothes and the slip of paper was valueless. Harsh, very harsh, words were said. Before becoming serious, the official backed down with an aggrieved expression twisting his face. Some fifteen minutes later we arrived at Manchester's Victoria station. There indeed was the train on the Through road awaiting us and preventing any movement on that line. Quickly we took our places. Suddenly, there was a hitch, my mate saying he would have to dash, as he was 'taken short'. *'Get at the regulator Jimmy,* he said. *'Keep going as slowly as you can'.* Off he sped. It must have been one of the quickest ever 'visits'. We never left station limits by the time he returned. We had around 35 vehicles on our tail and the train was a heavy one. We were sidelined a couple of times before reaching Bolton where the booked relief had

arrived. By that time, each of us had achieved a 'turn' out of the job. We finished the day shunting about the shed working to the foreman's instructions. Looks can be deceptive and non more so than loss of hair. One passed fireman had become totally bald on top by age thirty-three. One of the cleaners not known for intellect was sent with a note from the Running Foreman asking the passed man to sign on for driving. When the mans much younger looking wife answered the door he blurted out, *'Would you give this to yer dad please?'* As recounted elsewhere there were occasions when signals relating to another running line and set at clear were mistakenly passed. An example of this occurred during February of 1965. A Black Five No. 45378 was returning to Bolton light engine from Wigan. At Crowe Nest Junction they were run into the loop to let another train pass them. Running at reduced speed, but seeing the main line signal go to clear the driver obviously forgot that they were in the loop and put on steam. The effects were that they smashed through the buffers at the end of the loop, demolished a platelayer's shelter and ran into the abutment of an overbridge. There the engine came to a sudden violent stop, tilting at a grotesque angle. A day or so later, a group of locomen were discussing the incident in the drivers lobby. On the other side of the

I never did have a trip on one of these elderly L&Y 2-4-2 tanks. The nearest I got was a ride to Horwich Works off Bolton shed when sent on an errand for spares for the foreman fitter. I guess though that they sounded much the same as an 'A' class when opened up and 'fire drawing' took place. On the 22nd of February 1953, **50764** is at Lostock Hall shed. The engine was transferred to Low Moor - Bradford (25F) shortly after and saw out her days there before being withdrawn in July 1956.   *M J Blackburn*

The 5/40pm Manchester Victoria to Blackburn is crossing the Croal viaduct just beyond Bradshawgate. Perhaps it was just around this point that the fireman lobbed the makeshift 'jimmy' over the viaduct and into the Croal. In the right background can be seen Trinity Street station clock and further to the right the spires of Trinity church are boldly visible. Just to the right of the viaduct, Bradshawgate box can be seen. It is Friday May 17th 1963 and many of the products advertised are still available forty years on.

E M Bentley

room a driver, puffing thoughtfully on his pipe, was listening to the discussion. On hearing that the engine would probably be withdrawn as a result of damage sustained, and showing no thought for the safety of the Black Fives crew, or indeed if anyone in the hut had been harmed, asked with a most deadpan face, *'Is it one of our best?'* One driver, often on early morning turns boasted a swan's egg in his serge jacket pocket. At Blackrod, the same chap spotted a hen by the side of the track that had been knocked about. Swiftly he nipped off the footplate and grabbed his 'find'. Sadly though, before he could wring its neck he had been spotted. The hen's real owners were on the platform waiting to recover the foolish fowl. Needless to say he was made to give it back. In my earlier books I have referred to the time in 1961 that I was on passenger work and firing for 'Happy' Harry Schofield. Harry was so nicknamed

because he seldom smiled. Most often his face wore a scowl. Although Harry was an L&Y man he had transferred to Plodder Lane shed on the L&NWR side of Bolton in order to become promoted to driver. One evening whilst at Plodder, he and his mate arrived on shed in the middle of a torrential downpour. They had been wrong way around for the weather on their Derby Four 0-6-0 class 4F and were soaked to the skin. After disposal of their engine they were booked to assist on shed, turning and shedding locos after the fire-droppers had done their bit. Because Harry lived near to the shed he said he would go home, get dried off, put on some dry clothes and return. Just to be sure he also provided himself with his wellies. By this time the shed yard was well and truly flooded and the tops of the rails were just about visible. Most of the outside inspection pits had been filled in because they were not needed. However, just one pit

had not so been treated. Harry, playing it safe, walked down the shed yard where he could see there were tracks. However, because he was not a native of Plodder Lane shed he was unaware of the one pit left un-filled. Splashing on, in his brand new wellies, blissfully ignorant of what awaited him, he walked straight into the flooded pit and received a thorough ducking. There are lots of stories about bacon and eggs being cooked in the firebox and then going up the chimney. Never though had I heard one about black puddings. One driver attached his two delicacies to a wooden stick and stuck them in the urn on top of the cooker from which staff made up their brew cans. They couldn't understand why their tea tasted so foul and was of an oily texture. Revenge was had when they found out the culprit. The same driver, borrowing a pan in which to cook his eggs, set out his stall ready to eat once the boiled eggs were cooked. On opening them, the whites, and the yolks were a rich blue colour. Someone had dropped a piece of indelible blue pencil into the water. Everything was blue, even the air. All the breakfast had to be slung, it was inedible. There are lots of other tales too short to refer to, save for a passing mention, such as the occasion when George Merry refused to take me, a passed cleaner, on the 7.18am to Liverpool and the first part of the 10.30am Liverpool to York express which we operated as far as Manchester. Only a couple of weeks previously I had fired on a 'short rest' turn to Morecambe. I couldn't see what all the fuss was about. I was eighteen and brim full of confidence. In George's book I was a cheeky young upstart and he wasn't having me as his fireman. I was substituted when his regular mate turned up L.O.D. Or of driving on Moses Gate pilot, aged 16 with an elderly 'A' class with 'Bransby' Williams aged a bit more than sixty. The stories that

Harry Holmes told me of firing on the 'Q.P.' at Horwich, the nickname for the C.M.Es personal Coupe, George Hughes then being the CME. Of Ernie Worral who worked during the 1955 strike and being actively dissuaded by others from speaking to him because of it. And of another occasion when a driver who had also worked during an ASLEF strike was 'jazzbanded' down the street on leaving the sheds. The 'accompaniment' used was neighbouring householders dust bin lids. Or of Bill Liddle, somewhat bandy legged and an avid member of the ambulance class at Bolton. During the hours of darkness, Bill would study his first aid manual by the light of the fire sat on an upturned bucket. Because of that he was aptly named 'bucket a-se'. There was Jim Bob Young who often said his chronically sick chest was always a lot better when he was working on a 2-6-4 tank. Its atmosphere suited him admirably. One driver who often liked a pint or two 'borrowed' his wife's savings out of the vase on the sideboard at his home. Or 'IPA' Jack who was also nicknamed the drunken monk. When on a pub-crawl and much the worse for wear he would often leap on the bar, put a penny over one eye and perform a dance routine. One of the most formal, matter of fact souls was Harry Harrison in the top passenger link in 1959. One Saturday afternoon during that wonderful hot summer, Harry and I were 'spare' on shed. Around two 'o' clock we were given the pleasant task of taking a 'Crab' light engine to Blackpool Central shed. The Mogul, 42942, had completed its trials after overhaul at Horwich and from Blackpool would work its way back to its home depot. During the run the bracelet on my wrist watch came apart. Harry surprised me by mending the bracelet on the way home passenger after disposing of the engine at Blackpool. April of 1965 brought about the closure of Bury shed and a lot of extra

work for Bolton. Twenty of what had been Bury's locos were absorbed into Bolton's stock, plus one 2-6-4 tank (42574) from Patricroft raising the total number of locos allocated to Bolton to 57. This equalled the figure it attained in August of 1953, the highest it would attain during BR days. On that memorable Monday of 1965, I started what was to be eighteen months working with Joe Strickleton on goods work. On the second day of working LY pilot at Bury I was placed in charge of cooking our bacon and eggs. Having over-cooked the bacon I was immediately 'sacked' and told to drive instead-marvellous!! From October of 1966 for a little over twelve months I had a lot of fun and laughs working with Wilf Faulkner. Although safety was never compromised we got up to a lot of tricks others might have scorned. One nice story though is of an occasion when we had not to show our face too soon back at Bolton shed for various reasons. In a few weeks time I was off to the Isle of Wight for a week's holiday. I needed some new socks, so, to lose some time Wilf and I went shopping in Bolton town centre. The market hall was our destination. The right stall was found and in no time at all I chose six pairs of navy blue, nylon/cotton socks. The assistant proceeded to wrap up the socks for me. Just as the finishing touches were being applied to the parcel Wilf laid his hand on that of the assistants and said. *'Oh, just a minute luv,'eed like ter try um all on fust'*. We knew so little about most of the chaps that we worked with. One thing is for sure, most of them were just ordinary blokes earning a living. Some did it better than others. A number of drivers were out and out 'thrashers' and knew little about the locos they drove and how to get the best from them. Others knew how to work expansively, coax the best out of a loco and save the fireman much back bending Those were the 'enginemen', not just 'drivers'. They were my heroes.

After undergoing heavy general repairs at Horwich, Stanier class 8F No. **48321** is on a running in turn on the 7.22am Haslams to Bullfield trip. The train is about to pass Bullfield East signal box with the gasholder of Bullfield gas works looming large in the background. Hanging out of the cab nearest camera is fireman David Sharrock and driver Bob Croston. The date is around April / May 1960. *Lionel Hills*

(Right-page 23) Getting to grips with Westhoughton bank on a Liverpool to Rochdale working is BR Standard class 4MT 4-6-0 No.75047. Here, on this climb, one of the Aspinall 2-4-2 tanks slipped itself to a stand resulting in the episode related in chapter two. *T Heavyside*

(Above) At Bolton shed, sometime between 1962 and 1964, a group takes a breather for a camera session. Seated on the left on the footplating of Black Five No. **45290** is driver Tommy Sammon, whilst in front of him is passed fireman Harold Howarth. To their right are a couple of fitters not identified. The engine on the extreme right is an Ivatt 2-6-0 on trial from Horwich works. The Ivatt's tender carries a guard rail in connection with the 25Kv overhead equipment. *courtesy S A Leyland*

(Above-right) Lostock Junction station on July 18th 1963 and a special rail motor has been provided as a connection for day-trippers homeward bound for Horwich from Southport. Standing on the platform is driver Joe Maestri. Joe's father was of Italian origin and followed the trade of a scissor grinder. Standing in the gangway door of BR class 2MT 2-6-2 tank No. **84013** is fireman Maurice Heppolette. Seated on the fireman's seat, enthusiast Bert Mather has infiltrated. *D Hampson*

(Left) On the right of camera, George Glover stands in the gangway door of Plodder Lane's Ivatt 2-6-2 tank No. **41216**. When redundancies occurred owing to the closure of Plodder Lane depot George transferred to Patricroft rather than move to the 'other side'. Still later he became a postman. Seated is driver W.Heywood of Plodder Lane depot. *courtesy G Glover*

(Right) Just why ex L&Y 2-4-2 tank No. **50850** is on number 3 road at Bolton is unclear since locos were often placed here prior to entering factory. In this May 1959 portrayal she is not in steam and no evidence exists of her entering Horwich at that time. In April of 1954 a heavy general was afforded to her along with a new boiler. After that the engine ran only 164 miles before being placed in store for twelve months. In 1957, 857 miles were covered whilst in 1960, 14,624 miles were run. In the year of withdrawal 1961, as the last of the class, 2,510 miles were run and throughout the engines lifetime of sixty-two years, 1,496,826 miles were covered. *D Hampson*

(Centre) Now that the diesels were here, steam had to share its stabling point with them. Alongside Hunslet diesel shunter, LMS Standard 0-6-0 class 3F shunting tank No. **47202** is caught in an undignified pose with her coupling rods down, at the bottom of number two road on October 8th 1964. *H L Holland*

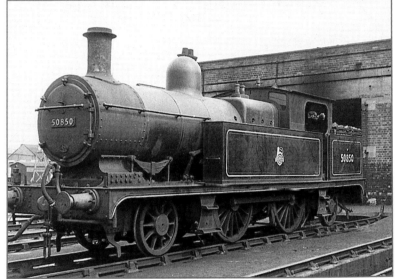

(Below) By the time this photograph was taken in March of 1963 we were gradually swapping our two cylinders for the sixteen or so of the diesel electric. The Sunday, 9.50am Manchester Victoria to Blackpool Central and North is entrusted to a Type 4 English Electric loco. The nine coaches would not present too much of a challenge for this 2,000 Hp unit. The train is passing Bullfield West on the outskirts of Bolton on the Down Fast line. *E F Bentley*

(Right-upper) When a hen was set loose on the railway line at Blackrod, the rail motor driver's attempts at procuring it for the cooking pot were thwarted when the real owners asked for it back In this view, the 'pegs' are up indicating it is almost time for **50646** to push her featherweight load back up the bank to Horwich. No date for this scene, but the radial was at Bolton during the earlier part of 1951 for a couple of months before going to Royston. *N R Knight*

(Right-centre) To say my old mate Harry Schofield was sometimes unlucky is an understatement. 'Happy' Harry seldom smiled and was always unlucky. In my earlier book I told of an incident when we ran into the back of a standing light engine causing quite a bit of damage. On the occasion I am about to relate you could say he was doubly unlucky. By origin, Harry was an L&Y man starting at Crescent Road depot. In order to get booked a driver a little more quickly he transferred to Plodder Lane. One afternoon during a heavy rainstorm Harry arrived on Plodder shed on a Derby Four wrong way round for the weather, soaked through. After shedding their engine, Harry and his fireman were to assist the fire droppers, stabling each engine as it was dealt with. After seeing to his own loco, Harry went to his home which was quite near at hand to dry off and put on dry, clean clothing. As an added measure, he also put on his wellies. Making his way down the flooded shed yard in his clean dry overalls and new wellies he played safe walking between the tracks, the tops of which were just visible. Most of the oiling pits had been filled in, but just one had not been so treated. Harry was unaware of that. Unfortunately, he picked just that one as he blissfully strode on for his swimming lesson, almost up to his shoulders in greasy water! In this view, Derby Four No. **44505** is almost ready for steaming at Horwich works after what looks like a general repair. The date is June 17th 1962. *Paul Claxton*

(Above) This 'Crab' 2-6-0 has just banked a Brindle Heath to Carlisle freight and is now galloping back to Bradshawgate ready for its next job. Harry Harrison is just about visible at the controls. In the background is Walton's Siding box. Harry surprised me one afternoon during 1959 by mending my watch bracelet after we had taken 42942 to Blackpool Central. *Authors collection*

For some reason, George Merry, pictured here, a top link driver until his retirement in 1961, had me marked down as a cheeky young seventeen year old and he wasn't going to have me as his fireman. Luckily for George (and me), his own fireman turned up L.O.D and was put on to his own turn. *courtesy Bert Welsby*

(Above-left) Eighteen happy months were spent firing for driver Joe Strickleton from April 1965 until October of 1966. On the first day we worked together, he even sacked me from cooking the bacon. Marvellous, that meant more time spent driving steam engines. In this scene, Joe is at the regulator of Black Five No. **5000** on the Severn Valley line during preservation times. *courtesy the Strickleton family* **(Above-right)** When this picture was taken, there were only a matter of days left to steam at Bolton shed. The author, pictured to the left, was in no doubt about the future without steam, on the railways for me there was **no** future ! Wilf Faulkner on the right had been my driver from October of 1966 until the same month in 1967. From that time onwards, we worked together from time to time. Always a 'rebel', Wilf is casually dressed whilst I have acquired a diesel drivers hat. *Jack Duxbury*

Originally a Wigan L&Y man, Jack Ashcroft transferred to Bolton in the early sixties. Jack is pictured aboard a Stanier 2-6-4 tank in this clear shot. *J Ashcroft*

(Left) Neil Grundy, pictured here aboard a type 90 electric locomotive is almost ready to depart from Euston with the 2/30pm to Glasgow during 1988. When I started my railway career in January of 1956, Neil was already a passed cleaner. *Neil Grundy*

(Right) One of the smartest turned out firemen was Fred Sharrock, here at the controls of a type 4 diesel electric locomotive many years after the withdrawal of steam. There was always a super shine on Fred's clogs, and his overalls always had that just washed look. Perhaps one day he will let me in on his secret of keeping so clean. *Neil Grundy*

CHAPTER THREE
THE MEN IN CHARGE

Darlington works has repaired Stanier class 8F No.48652. The 2-8-0, which arrived from Darlington on the 10th/11th June 1965, carries the larger style of cab side lettering whilst the power classification is omitted. These were some of the men "in charge". On the left, Jack Kay was principally a telephone attendant who occasionally deputized for the foreman cleaner. Wilf Bottomley a former driver was telephone attendant. I don't remember Wilf working a midnight shift, he had a medical condition which could have prevented that. Third from the left is Arthur Hulton affectionately nicknamed 'Flashbulb' because of his somewhat erratic nature. Arthur was one of the running foremen who arranged the power. Lastly, Mr. Jim Axford the shed superintendant. For a number of years prior to this post Jim had been leading fitter at Bolton. He was therefore, well known and addressed by everyone by his first name, never, I'm sure disrespectfully. *courtesy Bert Welsby*

It came as a surprise to youngsters of fifteen, as I then was, to learn that those chaps who were in charge of us, such as foremen cleaners, would be retiring in two or three years time. We seldom cleaned more than one engine in a shift. If we were found doing nothing we were simply sent back to scrape some more of the grime from the engine side rods. Cleaning engines didn't seem too high a priority. In a few months many of us would be passed for firing duties as we turned sixteen years of age. Shift work too from that point onwards would be the order of the day. During 1957, in Bristol, British Railways were fined for employing people under the age of eighteen years on shifts they were not supposed to be on. The practice continued even after the case had been heard and judgement delivered. That rule, it seemed, could be broken and then forgotten. Daily, by a notice posted on the inside of the drivers lobby door we were reminded by rule 15 that we must not walk on the line. Regrettably, one passed cleaner who chose to ignore this rule (as we all did) was knocked down by the shed top points as he walked to work. Sadly, a hand was severed and lost. Some of the times we started at were 12.30(midnight), 4.00am and an awful one I always hated, 6.00pm, because others were going home just about the time we were travelling to

work. We needed constant watching by the foreman cleaner. We were supposed to be cleaning engines. One lad who escaped his watchful eye lost part of a finger, and almost his footplate career whilst helping the 7.30am shed men during shunting operations, trapping the finger between buffers whilst using a shunt pole. There were two foreman cleaners. One was on the 8.00am shift and he supervised all the shed staff, cleaners and labourers, but not those on the fitting or artisan side. His counterpart would be on the12.00 (midnight) shift. On that turn the role consisted of telephone attendant. One of the main duties was handing out time cards to those signing on and off duty. It was often this assistant who notified us of which engines we were to prepare. Sometimes he was referred to as the Running Shift Foreman's assistant. When the day foreman cleaner was off for a weeks leave others would be promoted to work 'vice' him. Often, the task would fall to an ex-loco man. These were chaps who, for medical reasons had come off footplate work and had been found other jobs labouring. When those men caught us 'lobbing' or doing nothing, we were directed to the mess room for a cup of tea rather than just hang about. After a brew we were kindly told to get back to the business of cleaning engines, and we were constantly being reminded

that we were actually being paid for all this. When there came a change of Motive Power Department Superintendent, or Shed master, all of us were on our guard. As time went on we learnt that perhaps the new individual didn't know as much as he was 'cracked up' to know. Often, when some of the cleaners were promoted on to labouring, he would spend ages asking what job we were doing. Having been provided with a brush, a square mouthed shovel and a wheelbarrow, it should have been obvious we were sweeping up! How exactly it came to light I don't really know, but he had become nicknamed the 'million dollar fitter' during an apprenticeship at Horwich Works, earlier in his career. It is well known that at Bolton, we trialled engines that had received repairs at Horwich Locomotive Works. After General repairs, some of them seemed to be around close on a month before they were released back to their home depots. There were occasions too when some of the motionwork was reassembled with too little tolerance, which could cause problems once the engine was back in revenue earning service. Amongst the various classes of loco dealt with at Horwich we frequently encountered the class four 2-6-0s of Ivatts design, those numbered 43000-43161. I particularly liked to work on these

The Ivatt 2-6-0s of power classification 4MT were, for me, exciting engines to work on. You were sat high up with the valve gear all visible and a clear view ahead. However, they did need careful firing because like the Derby Fours their fireboxes sloped very steeply at 1:4. Most times you placed the coal under the door and in the back corners letting it 'gravitate' to the front. Here, the doyen of the class, No. **43000** takes life at a leisurely pace whilst running in after repairs at Horwich on station pilot duty at Blackpool Central station. The date is June 20th 1961. *Frank Dean*

machines, preferring them to the BR product of equal power which always seemed as if they needed a kick to get them on the road. On occasion however, they presented some problems. In 1958, as a passed cleaner I had 'failed' with one of them on a special to Southport. We had to make an emergency stop at Parbold with a broken valve spindle on number 43010. On another occasion, around twelve months later, one of these Moguls was on trial at Bolton after general repairs at Horwich. Almost at the end of the shift, the engine was operating a short freight working from Halliwell to Burnden. The freight was signalled on to the Up through line from the Blackburn direction. As the engine was passing Bolton West signal box on the sharp leftwards curve the short slide bars which guided the valve rod seized. With the left hand valve suddenly stopping but the rest of the motion keeping on moving, most of the motion bent like hairpins with the loco stopping double quick. With the train blocking all the Up roads, all traffic in that direction was brought to a complete standstill. All the bent components had to be removed before any movement of the engine and its train could take place. To say there was delay to all trains in the Up direction is understating the case. To say that great attempts were made to lay the blame at someone's feet is also an understatement. A little over a week previously the engine had been trialled by one of the crews stationed at Horwich for that purpose. Two days before the incident, the other driver stationed at Horwich brought the 2-6-0 to Bolton to enter traffic. As was usual, they disposed of and shedded the engine. They then returned to Horwich. The day after the incident, the same driver brought another engine to Bolton to enter traffic. On ringing in to the foreman's office he was given orders to report to the shed superintendent 'immediately'. This

particular driver had had a couple of 'brushes' with the new superintendent but knew nothing of the incident with the Ivatt. On reaching the front office, he found the official hopping mad and in a gloating mood, thinking he would have his own back on the footplateman. The official believed he now had the 'upper hand' and demanded an instant report and charged the driver with responsibility for the whole matter. Far from being put out, the driver said yes he would oblige with a full report. However, as others had both handled and trialled the Mogul, they too must be asked for their versions. The driver also suggested to the official, for whom he had an intense dislike, that it should be obvious that the slide bars had been put up with too little tolerance. But if he was expected to check such matters he would want to be provided with a micrometer. He would then need to be trained adequately how to use it and be paid a lot more money. After all that, the official backed down. When the examining fitter

said that the other side had no clearance and would soon have seized, there the matter ended. The works, it seemed was at the root of the problem. On another occasion, the same official was on duty when a Blackpool engine failed at Burnden. The engine, a Black Five was brought down over the ash pit and behind the shed near to the Running Shift Foreman's office. There, the motion was set. In the presence of the leading fitter and the shed master the valves and pistons were tested. All was not well 'It's alright', said the superintendent to the accompaniment of a roar up the chimney. There were in fact, twelve broken rings!

(Below) In my first book I described how I had 'failed' with a broken valve spindle with Ivatt class 4, 2-6-0 No. 43010 on a Southport excursion. Perhaps that was also an occasion when Horwich had assembled the spindles with too little tolerance. Here, the same loco is operating a stopping passenger train at Evesham during 1956. *R W Hinton*

(**Right**) Signing on for cleaning at 4.00am on the 15th of April 1958, I never dreamed that I would be told to take 40680 along with sister engine 40681, (pictured here) to Derby works. I actually made it all the way to the works and ended up signing off around 4/00pm with a 'twelver' under my belt. The 4-4-0 is pictured approaching Cherry Tree Junction on the line to Blackburn.   *courtesy S Taylor*

Bolton shed, where I lived out my comparatively short railway career could hardly be regarded as a major cog in British Railways wheel. The average distance of most of the sheds workings would be about thirty-five miles. Southport, Liverpool, Blackpool, Wakefield and Hellifield were regularly visited. There were also journeys made whilst running light engine. One odd trip which I was most fortunate to make was with one of the LMS class 2P super-heaters to Derby works. Wigan sheds' No. 40680 had arrived on Bolton shed during the evening of April 14th 1958. Signing off at lunchtime that day after a spell of engine cleaning, I had checked the daily alter-ations list to see if I was marked for firing the next day. My name was nowhere to be seen, so I would be engine cleaning again. Imagine my surprise, signing on next day at 4.00am, to be told to book on for firing and to get 40680 ready with Wilf Faulkner and to take her to Derby works. Collision damage was to be put right. By sheer coin-cidence, one of our own class 2P super-heaters, No. 40681 had also been accepted for shopping at Derby for general repairs. The two 4-4-0s were to travel, coupled together, in steam all the way to Derby. It must have been quite an expensive trip. Two sets of men, both need-ing conductors which were supplied all the way to Derby by Newton Heath depot. That didn't worry me though. I was keen to break new ground and would have some-thing different to tell the rest of the clean-ing gang next day. We were sidelined a number of times and arrival on Derby Works was not until lunchtime. I signed

off duty with just about twelve hours under my belt that day. Some drivers at Bolton had excellent route knowledge and on occasion one could enjoy a change of scenery. When one of our class four tanks at Bolton was accepted for repairs at Crewe works the driving duties were entrusted, on one particular occasion, to Tommy Jordan. He was able to go all the way to the works. At about the same time, there had been complaints from the works that far too much coal was being left in the bunker or tender. To avoid waste, this had to be shovelled off and loaded into wagons so it could be used. There was therefore only a minimal amount of coal on board which was considered sufficient to get the loco to Crewe. On boarding the loco, both driver and fireman viewed coal stocks suspiciously when noting how little coal had been left for the journey. Another instruction received from the works was that the engine must carry a full complement of fire irons and that a footplate brush must be provided. Eventually, eyeing the coal somewhat doubtfully they set off with all instruc-tions complied with. Needless to say, waste of coal and water was avoided. Arriving at Manchester Victoria, they were brought to a stand on the Through road. Ahead, they saw that freight had 'stuck' on Miles Platting bank. There was no banker available. They were, therefore, commandered by control to assist the luckless freight. Bearing in mind the minimal amount of coal at their disposal, the absolute minimum of pushing was done. The job was stopped so they had no

alternative. The pushing cut very deeply into the already depleted stock of coal. The fireman, to quote his own words 'put coal on the fire like a chap without arms'. Many miles before reaching Crewe, it was painfully obvious that they were going to run out of coal. Stopping on the main line at a signal box, some coal was 'borrowed' from its coal bunker. After about ten minutes shovelling they had to move on, a train was approaching the section in rear. Just for sheer devilment, the fireman went into the locos bunker and swept out all that remained. In sight of Crewe Works they were held up on a goods loop. Now, with no coal at all and with the fire very low they considered throwing it out. Nearby, some trenches had been dug. Around and about them lay the scrap timber which had been used to shore up with. These were scrounged, luckily there being no workmen around at the time. They proved to be their salvation and just about kept the fire going until coming to rest on the works arrival road. A huge, red-faced official now stormed up to the foot-plate. *'Don't you dare get off that footplate 'till I've seen how much coal's left in that bunker. If there's too much you can get back to Bolton with it'.* Hearing this verbal onslaught, the driver politely asked him to come and have a look and make his own mind up. Seeing the swept out bunker, he was stuck for words and was good enough to apologize for the harsh tones. He explained to the two Bolton men how much of a problem it was emptying a large amount of coal and then wheel-barrowing it away. There was never any trouble like that at Horwich. The working of rest days was a means of vastly increasing one's take home pay. The rate paid was usually time and a half. If a full eight hours was worked during daytime hours, one would be paid for twelve hours. Occasionally, the job for which a set of men was marked might be a short working, perhaps only six hours. The total then credited would be nine hours. Sometimes, overtime would mean a bumper days pay. When the re-furbishment of Darcy Lever viaduct was taking place in 1958, I was marked to work my Saturday rest day. Signing on time was 10.00pm on the Saturday night. With the National Agreements as they then stood, between the hours of midnight on the Saturday, and 6.00am on the Sunday double time was the order of the day. Between 10.00pm and midnight the rate was time and three quarters. The following week, my pay would be boosted by a massive fifteen hours! The working stands out boldly in my memory. That evening, our engine was class 7F, 'Austin Seven' No. 49618 which at that time had only been off the shops, following a general overhaul, for a matter of six months. She was in the pink, and it was probably one of the easiest turns I ever had. Because those engines had no vacuum equipment, and possessed only a steam brake, very little water was used. After we had got our train in place for the engineers, we only moved twice during the whole of our shift. A similar thing happened about a year later when a 'deep dig' was taking place at Blackrod on the line to Preston. On that occasion, strange to relate, our seating arrangements were not as comfy as those of the 'Austin Seven'. On the latter occasion we had an ex works 'Stanier Crab' on the turn. With their seats tucked into the cab-side sheeting you could only sit on half of the seat. Signing on duty one Thursday morning during 1962, a set of men from the top goods link noted they had been marked to work their rest day the next day. Disappointingly, the job was only a short one. They were to prepare an engine, run light to Horwich where they would back on to seven corridor coaches. From there, they were to run empty to Bury where they would pick up a party of schoolchildren. From there, the last port of call was Midland Junction. At that point, they would uncouple and an electric locomotive would whisk the train over the

The '**Austin Sevens**' were strong engines, too strong for their light construction so they became very badly run down quite quickly. **49618**, pictured here entering the coal road at Bolton shed on 21st March 1958 is only a couple of months into its general overhaul at Horwich of January 1958. *D Hampson*

Pennines to the East Coast. They were then booked back, light engine to Bolton shed to dispose of the engine and finish. Several hours later, on the day before the trip, and whilst in the drivers lobby to sign off duty, the running foreman told them he had 'tagged' another job on to the trip. After the schools party trip, they were to return light to Horwich, this time to the works to move some electric stock, after overhaul, to Altrincham, where it would re-enter traffic. The extra job would mean an hour or so overtime, but no arguing (as if they would), because there was no-one else to do the job. A further point was that the only power available would be an ex works 'Crab' which had not yet

completed its running in period from Horwich. The engine must come back to Bolton on completion. They had not, under any circumstances to be relieved. This particular foreman, Jack Coar, was not one for putting overtime on the cards, but this time it was the only solution. The following morning, the driver and fireman signed on for the first part of the turn. Just to re-enforce the point, there was a note pinned to the drivers card reminding them that they must bring the engine back to Bolton and had not to be relieved. Control had been advised about the arrangements. Everything went well with the first part of the turn. However, arriving at Horwich works, the crew were advised that the

Heavy power here for the morning Moses Gate pilot which is standing on the fork line at the Rose Hill end awaiting a road into Rose Hill sidings. Passed cleaner Trevor Partington is in the cab of 49544. This Austin was withdrawn at Horwich works in February of 1960. *D Hampson*

The end of the line for a couple of 'Austin Sevens'. **49668** and **49618**, (goodness knows which is which), have arrived at Thompson's wagon works at Ince near Wigan for breaking up. It was a pity that these locos were ill equipped mechanically because they would steam and were strong engines. With only seven full turns of the reverser from full forward to full back gear they were handier when shunting was the order of the day than the Stanier machine of 8F. But so far as anything else goes, they weren't in with a shout. *Paul Claxton*

electric stock was not quite ready. They would have to wait a short while. This short while went on for rather a long while. The drivers route knowledge extended only as far as Ardwick Junction where a conductor was arranged. The guard, a Manchester Victoria based man was already on long hours. His relief was promised on arrival at Manchester 'Vic'. Eventually, the short train got under way via Bolton and stopped on the Through road at Manchester Victoria for the guards relief. As usual, there was no relief. The guard, now on well over twelve hours was all for walking off the job. That would have left them stranded. Control now promised the man certain relief at Ardwick Junction where the train must stop anyway for a conductor driver. Of course, there was no relief for the guard there either, so the man walked off the job. Before arriving back at Manchester Vic to sign off he would have been on duty in excess of fifteen hours. It was now after 4.30pm so the driver telephoned control about the conductor driver and a replacement guard. On speaking to the controller, the saga had now reached fantasy land. The man at Hunts Bank told the driver that his information was that the engine was an 'experimental' one and that this driver was the only man competent to handle it. There was no conductor until 6.00pm and no guard available until 6.30pm. Please would he hang on. To explain to the controller that the engine was an ordinary works repair trials loco would have been tedious. Instead, the driver agreed to hang on with one proviso. That was that he was able to go into the street below and stock up with fish and chips or similar. The controller agreed and a supply of the best meat and potato pies was found and a stock brought on to the footplate. The conductor driver, and relief guard duly arrived and the delayed train moved off from Ardwick Junction at 6.45pm. After the stock had been put away at Altrincham they were faced with a very long journey back to Bolton, tender first. Between the three of them, they travelled to Castlefield Junction, and then engine first to Ordsall Lane. From there, the conductor driver didn't know any further, but the regular driver was alright from that point onwards to Bolton shed where they booked off at 9.45pm with about sixteen hours duty. A sad end to the tale was that the driver's wife wasn't pleased when he turned up without his pay, the office having been closed many hours before he signed off. A week later she was delighted though with the size of the pay packet after the very fruitful rest day! For a number of years, at Bolton, we had a working, which we knew simply as 'the fish'. This job was actually turn number 304F for which we booked on at 5.25pm. The engine was prepared for us, so once the notices had been read and the shovel and bucket of tools had been withdrawn from the stores, we took ourselves off to our engine and departed from the shed at 5.40pm. Over the fork line we went to 'B' side, (Rose Hill Sidings) where our train awaited us, the 6.05pm freight to Moston. On occasion, there might be a few fitted vans next to the engine. The train loaded to around forty vehicles. After disposing of the train at Moston, some time would be spent

Of the two varieties of 'Crabs', the Stanier machine was the more modern and was of course Staniers first effort after taking up residence at Crewe. The fireman's seat was tucked away far too close to the cab side sheeting and you could only get one cheek on it. **42975** stands at Bolton shed whilst on trial after repairs at Horwich loco works. The date is August 5th 1960.   *N E Preedy*

shunting there until a 9.05pm departure for Dewsnap. The final part of the turn involved the working of a parcels train from Ashton Moss from the East coast with fish vans attached. Hence the name 'the fish'. On one occasion in the later 1950s, power was in short supply. All that was available was an 'Austin' class 7F 0-8-0. All went well until the train was being coupled up at Ashton Moss. The working was a class C freight, fully braked on all vehicles. Because the 0-8-0 possessed no vacuum equipment, the wires had to be drawn on the vehicles in order to release the brakes. The driver instructed his fireman to put class 'H' lamps up on the smokebox, through freight. All was now ready for departure. Or was it? The foreman wired the train away via the adjacent signal box but the outlet signal was not raised. Quite some time passed. The foreman rang the signalman to ask why the train was being held, whereupon he suggested he ask the driver why the train had not yet left as he was carrying the wrong headlamps. The driver now went to the signalbox to speak to the signalman. The man's greeting to the driver was somewhat irate, *'Tha nows why I've not pulled off for yer, yerv got the wrong lamps on and am not pullin' off till they're put reet'.* When the driver told the 'Bobbie' why the lamps were set as they were his face went ashen and he quickly

set the points for the outlet road. There was nothing unusual about moving a diesel multiple unit to Reddish Electric Depot for wheel re-profiling. There, a marvellous machine could complete the job without removing the wheels from the unit very quickly indeed. Only a few weeks after passing out to drive DMUs a driver was sent to Bolton station to carry out such a mission on a Monday morning in the early 1960s.The twin set was standing on the Up pit in the station yard at Bolton Trinity Street. Arriving at the failed unit, which had operated a train

from Colne the previous Saturday, the driver found that the hand brake in the rear cab had been left hard on. In this manner, the wheels had simply been skidding all the way to Bolton. On discovering this at Bolton, the unit had been shunted into its resting place. The flats were quite spectacular and the C&W examiner refused to allow it to go. The examiner's immediate superior officer was sent for to see what he thought. He said the unit could go, but speed had not to exceed ten miles per hour. Where points and crossings were involved, the unit had to 'inch' its way through, dead slow. This meant that the train must be sidelined into every loop to let delayed passenger trains pass it. Progress was very slow. By the time Reddish had been reached, and the driver travelled home 'on the cushions' he had made well over twelve hours. Occasionally, those of us who were of an observant nature might get into trouble quite accidentally because of it. Ballast trains could take the loco crews into many varied places. That depended on where work was to be carried out. It was often the case however that when the ballast or materials train was in position there might be no movement called for over a long period of time. Seated there on the footplate, one still needed to be observant. The passing trains often were the only source of interest to keep one occupied. Many of us would know exactly the composition and order of trains. Furthermore, those more observant would notice anything out of the ordinary. During the early 1950s, Bolton ballast

Getting nicely run in after repairs at Horwich, Straight Framed Crab No. **42978** operates a Down coal train past Weeton Woods on April 25th 1957.
          Frank Dean

A much better proposition, so far as seating was concerned were the older 'Crabs' of Hughes design. With their one legged stool you could adopt any position you chose and were just as comfortable when running tender first. Bury sheds' **42820** is pictured as she leaves Blackpool Central with a return special for Oldham on July 12th 1962.
Frank Dean

was working at Chorley. For a time, the permanent way men were at lunch. All was quiet so far as 'ops' were concerned. It was a fairly hot day during the summertime and the crew of the ballast engine were indeed watching the trains as they passed by. Eventually, a train composed of empty fish vans passed en route to Fleetwood. The ballast train crew was well aware from past observations that the vans were always empty ones. On this particular day though, there was a very unusual, large van in the formation which was carried on two four wheeled bogies. A sliding door on the offside was pushed slightly open. Standing in the opening could be seen a very scruffy, tattered looking individual who it was felt should not be there at all. Thoughts sprang to their mind such as escaped convicts from Strangeways prison. After a short deliberation, the fireman went to the signal box to report what had been seen so that the police could meet the train at Preston. That was the end of the episode for that day. Booking on duty the following day for the same turn, the men were greeted by the telephone attendant. The unusual van on the fish empties had been added by special arrangement. The vehicle contained an elephant, and the dark skinned, scruffy looking person witnessed was the elephant's keeper. It would therefore, be in everyone's interest if the fireman kept his nose out of other

people's business in future! From 1962 onwards, on the withdrawal of through Colne-London services, we did have a small train that left Bolton at 4.52pm for Stockport where it made a connection with a train from Manchester Piccadilly bound for London. But could anything sound more unlikely that a Daisy Hill to London special. Even the power was unspectacular, a class four, 2-6-4 tank from the shed's own stud of locos. The turn took the men light to Horwich carriage sidings where they coupled up to seven corridor coaches. Then, running empty stock, their route took them via the direct line to Horwich Fork Junction, Hilton House, Dobbs Brow Jcn. and on to Daisy Hill, the first stop. From thence -forward all stops over the Atherton line to Manchester Victoria. Swinton Rugby League Football Club were playing in a Wembley cup final. At Manchester, the seven coaches were coupled to more coaches for the trip to London. Our men trundled off quietly back to Bolton shed to dispose of and shed the engine. The F.A Cup Final of 1960 brought together in the tie Blackburn Rovers and Wolverhampton Wanderers. Blackburn were the losers in an unfortunate encounter which saw one of their players, Dave Whelan, break a leg. The final score was 3-0 in Wolves' favour. The match brought a little work our way at Bolton and I booked on at 10.00pm with passed

fireman Jack Cleary to double head one of the return specials up the bank to Blackburn. Power for the working was a works trial engine, a 'Crab' 2-6-0 having undergone intermediate repairs at Horwich. The 'Crabs' figured a lot during the years Horwich was repairing them. Often, specials were powered by these able, easy to fire Moguls of Hughes design. The turn was a little unusual in that when all the despondent supporters had left the train at Blackburn and the headlamps changed to empty stock, we then carried on towards Rose Grove with the ten bogies and striking off to the right at Gannow Junction we took the steep line via Burnley Manchester Road, Portsmouth and Cornholme to Todmorden. At Stansfield Hall we took the right fork on to the Calder Valley line in a westerly direction. From that point we ran on via Rochdale, Bury and Bolton to Horwich carriage sidings, doing a complete circle. In my minds eye, I can still see that fire on our Mogul burning brightly as we blasted our way up past Holme where the gradient is 1:68. It wasn't often that Bolton men worked on the Patriot class. We had a regular turn to Liverpool with one of our own tank engines. There, we swapped footplates with Bank Hall men to work the 10.30am express with ten bogies for York and Newcastle, which we operated as far as Manchester Victoria. Often we encountered Bank Hall's....*continued on page 35*

(Left) Five of the Crabs were selected for experimental purposes by the fitting of Lentz rotary cam poppet valve gear. LMS No.**13124** is seen here so fitted. An indicator shelter is carried whilst operating a Manchester Victoria to Blackpool Central train via the Marton line. The line trailing in from the right is the old Preston & Wyre branch from Wrea Green. The date here is September 1932. *Frank Dean*

'CRABS' AT WORK

(Below) The Crabs were ideal power for this sort of work. With ten bogies on her tail, Rose Grove's **42869** takes the Padiham Loop line at Rose Grove West Junction and is about to descend the 1 in 40 incline with 1T80, the 10.27am Burnley to Blackpool Central period return. The date is July 1st 1961.
courtesy S Taylor

THURSDAY. BRITISH RAILWAYS										B.R. 87219		
19 APRIL 1962. ECS. Train from HORWICH.												
Engine No. 44346				Fireman's Name M. GLEESON.								
		Shunting Time			Loco. Our-Des away from H'me Shed	Time Lost by Loco.	Load		Delays		
STATIONS	Actual Time	Coaching	Freight	Depart-mental			Vehicles	Trans of Equiv No. of Wagons	Minutes	Cause	
	arr.	dep.	H. M.	H. M.	H. M.	Mins.	Mins.				
SHED		11.45									
HORWICH	12/10	2/0	1 15					3	35	NO TRAINS	
MIDLAND JN.		3/15									
ALTRINCHAM	4/0	5/0	1 - 0								
VIA											
HEATON M.		6/5									
CASTLETON		7/10									
BOLTON SHED		7/35									

REMARKS SIGNED OFF 7/45

8¾ HRS

(Above) Pocket notebooks were supplied to drivers in order that passing times could be noted and then transferred to the driver's ticket, which was completed at the end of the day. Just like the run in chapter four there was delay at Horwich. Nothing like the overtime encountered on that occasion though.

courtesy Bert Welsby

Continued from page 33..........un-named 45517. For the four days for which we were rosterred to do so, with a rest day taken on the Tuesday, I had the privilege of working on the 4-6-0 on just that turn. I can confirm that firing to the book, in short bursts with the firing plate in position she steamed well every day. The wonderful sound of "six beats to the bar" was music indeed. The chance of working on one of the re-built locos at Bolton was a little more remote. During the winter in the early part of 1960, I was doing nothing more challenging than sitting on 42626 on the station pilot at Bolton Trinity Street. The hands of the large clock on platform four near to the Down box where we stood with our 2-6-4 tank had crept round to a little after 3.05pm. The engine, which would operate the 3.50pm stopping train to Liverpool Exchange drew up alongside us on the Down goods loop. Surprisingly, this was re-built Baby Scott, class 7P No.45535, Sir Herbert Walker KCB. Even more surprising was the message that they were to exchange footplates with us! The later part of the diagramme would take the loco round the notorious Heywood curves, over which these locos were prohibited. What a swap! We took our places," Slinger" Wood and I on board the 4-6-0. By comparison the footplate seemed cavernous, and the firebox huge when compared to the tank. To save us from complete boredom on pilot duty, a trip to Horwich formed part of the job. Presently, we lumbered easily off first of all to the works to collect two stores vans. The 4-6-0 seemed outrageously large as it picked its way over the curves, points and crossings in the works yard. Eventually, we propelled our small train off the works yard out via Station Line to Horwich station. The leading stores van was shunted on to the vacant siding by the side of the platform road ready to be collected by the engine which would operate the 5/47pm departure to Manchester. Newton Heath was the first port of call for that stores van. Next, with the one stores van now attached to our Patriot, we backed on to our three-coach train ready to work the 4.54 to Bolton calling at Lostock Junction only. That day, we swept over Red Moss with our featherweight load and whisked our passengers into Bolton to the accompaniment of loud cheers from "spotters" on the footbridge which formerly spanned the station yard at Bolton. Not many "spotters" would be able to claim a "cop" like ours on the Horwich to Bolton stopper. In earlier times it would have produced nothing larger than an L&Y 2-4-2 "radial" tank. Once we had stabled the stock, and disposed of the stores van at Bolton we ran light to Bolton shed, Secretly, I hoped as many people as possible would see me that day aboard a re-built Patriot. Leaving the class 7P under the coal hopper for the 6.00pm disposal men to deal with, we walked down to the drivers lobby to sign off duty. I cast a whistful glance over my shoulder at 45535 with the light blue smoke curling nicely off the chimney top. How I wish we could have gone to Blackpool with her. But that's the stuff that dreams are made of! The 5/40pm Manchester Victoria to Hellifield express carried home a lot of people working at the railway offices at Hunts Bank. It was allowed just sixteen minutes from the Manchester start to its first stop at Bolton. Six minutes only were allowed to pass Clifton Junction. With some of the old hands it was a wild

"thrash" and often a late arrival at Bolton was clocked up. Just why it was so timed is not really clear; it was never a light train. Nine bogies were conveyed, four being uncoupled at Bolton to form the 6/08pm stopper, which followed to Blackburn. But on at least one occasion, nature took a hand in matters. During December of 1944, a well-known geological fault at Kearsley on the line of the Pendleton Fault caused a landslip. All services past the spot were suspended. The 5/40pm to Hellifield was run from Manchester Exchange non stop (in theory) to Bolton Great Moor Street. On arrival at the latter terminus, those going forward to Blackburn and beyond had to make a journey on foot across to Trinity Street. The first two days, six bogies were conveyed behind a side tank coal engine from Plodder Lane. On both occasions they had to stop for a "blow up". For the other three days Patricroft covered the temporary working with a Stanier tank.

(Right-upper) Passing Bradkirk on a Euston to Blackpool Central via the Marton line is re-built Patriot No. **45535**, *Sir Herbert Walker KCB*. On that run from Horwich we opened her up a bit and made good time over Red Moss. I can still hear the cheering from loco spotters on the bridge over the station yard as we negotiated Bolton West Junction into platform one at Trinity Street station.
Frank Dean

(Right-centre) All eyes on Trinity Street footbridge are on the 'namer', Jubilee No. **45601** *British Guiana*. The pilot engine, BR Class 4MT 2-6-0 No. **76077** of Sutton Oak shed, is a trials loco off Horwich Works. It had received light repairs and had been working out of Bolton. The date is August 18th 1962, and the train is the summer Saturdays only 9.20am Manchester Victoria to Glasgow Central via Blackburn and Hellifield. For many years, the bridge was a haven for train spotters and something of a 'short-cut' from Trinity Street into the town. Alas, it is now demolished. *courtesy N J Grundy*

(Right-lower) The 9.20am summer Saturdays only, Manchester Victoria to Glasgow Central via Blackburn and Hellifield has almost completed the stiff seven mile climb to the top of the bank at Waltons Siding on its way to Blackburn. Both engines are 'in the pink' with white feathers at the safety valves.
D Hampson

BOLTON TO ROCHDALE

During its heydey, Bolton Shed had a great number of turns both passenger and freight which took us along the route to Rochdale. The earliest of the passenger workings left Bolton at 5.15am. Very early on in my footplate career this was the first experience I had of passenger work. At that time, March 1957, we operated the train not only to Rochdale but around the line via Oldham to Manchester. We called it going 'round the houses'. The day ended with a quick run from Manchester, double heading the 9.30am Manchester to Glasgow train as far as Bolton. However, on a Saturday, the 5.15 ran only as far Rochdale, and after disposing of our train in Rochdale carriage sidings we ran light engine to Bolton shed to dispose of the engine. So, our pictorial journey starts alongside Bolton Trinity Street station's number 1 platform aboard 2-6-2T No 40072 with Driver Ralph Ainscough.

Standing at Bolton Trinity Street's number 1 platform, right where our journey to Rochdale begins, is Southport's 'Caprotti' Black Five No. **44743**. The date is September 3rd 1964, and the hands of the large clock on the platform decree it to be 8.45am. Although the engine seems to be in a very neglected state it actually survived for another sixteen months and a move in November of 1964 to Speke Junction shed. *courtesy S Taylor*

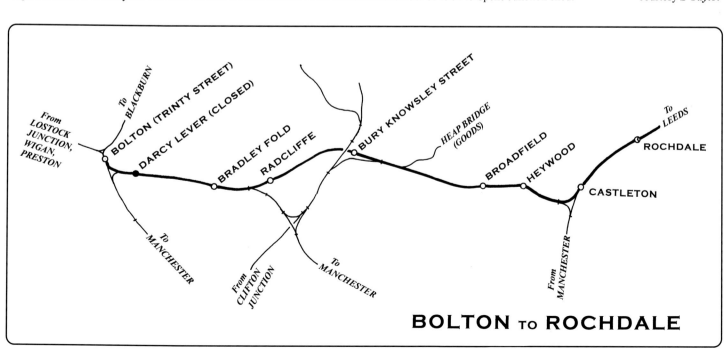

BOLTON TO ROCHDALE

(Above) Looking in the direction of travel, a Black Five is about to dive under Orlando Bridge and it is just possible to see the signals at clear for its passage on to the branch to Bury and Rochdale. The two locos are **44807** and **45272**. The date is March 25th 1964. *H L Holland*

(Below) On the 5th of June 1961, an ex L&Y 'A' class lifts one of the trips out of Haslams sidings for Bullfield which was on the west side of the station. **52523** was one of the last remaining 'A' classes at Bolton and was only withdrawn in September of the following year. The branch to Rochdale is to the left of the loco and its train. Only when we had rounded the curves and were passing Rose Hill Junction signal box would 40072 be given her head. *David Hampson*

(Above) By the time we were clattering over Darcy Lever viaduct the 'five-foot three-inch' drivers were turning at a fair pace. With Ralph Ainscough at the regulator just cracked into second valve and the reverser well notched up there was a well defined up and down thrust on board 40072 as we sped toward the gentle rise to Bradley Fold West. In this view, Stanier Class 8 No. **48740** of Bolton shed sets off tender first with a short train bound for Dobson & Barlow at Bradley Fold on 16/11/67. This viaduct and the one at Burnden were the first wrought iron lattice girder types in England when built in 1848. The girders were renewed in 1880/1. *E F Bentley*

(Right-centre) Approaching Bradley Fold West, an unidentified Ivatt Class 4MT 2-6-0 brings a fitted freight up the bank. Bradley Fold West has cleared his signal for the passage of the train. On the post can be seen what was known as a 'D' sign for a firemans call plunger. This indicated to the footplate crew that a press key was located at ground level so that in the event of coming to a stand at the signals the fireman could press the key located in a box by the signal which would cause an audible warning to be sounded in the signal box reminding the signalman of the presence of the train. No date for this scene which is thought to be around 1966/7. *P Salveson*

(Right-lower) One of Bolton shed's Stanier Class 8Fs No. **48504** lifts a rake of vans past Bradley Fold West 'box. Although the train appears to comprise fitted vans, the loco is carrying the headlamp code for express freight not fitted with continuous brake. The date again is around 1966/7. *P Salveson*

Two views from the platforms at Bradley Fold looking west towards Bolton. The footbridge (No 36 - numbered from Castleton) frames the level crossing and hiding behind it on the right is Bradley Fold Station signal box. We made our first stop here at 5.21am. **(Below)** Bradley Fold station marked the end of a section of the line from Bolton that contained Up and Down Loop lines and the bracket signals beneath the bridge indicate where the Up Loop converged to reconnect with the Up Main. In this view we can also see an L&Y veteran in the form of an 0-6-0 'A' Class loco shunting in the goods yard (cl. 1.8.63) which had a capacity for 76 wagons. Note also the quaint gas lamp hung on the corner of the building above the station entrance. Both views date from 7/11/50 prior to reconstruction of the footbridge. The station was given a facelift in 1968 when Her Majesty Queen Elizabeth II visited the factory of Dobson and Barlow. Closure came amid public outcry in October 1970 following withdrawal of the Bolton/Rochdale passenger trains. *Authors collection*

(Above) At Bradley Fold Junction, about a mile from Bradley Fold Station, the line to Radcliffe Central via Ainsworth Road Halt (cl. 21.9.53) branched off to the right. Using this route it was possible to run via Radcliffe North and West Junctions to Bury Loco Junction and the Bury Loop as well as Bolton Street station. Here in this July 4th 1965 portrayal, Bolton's Black Five No. **44664** is operating the 11.20am excursion from Rochdale to Blackpool North. The route to Radcliffe Central (as well as the connection between North and West Junctions had closed completely on the 2nd November 1964, although track and associated fixtures and fittings still await disposal.   (Below) About three quarters of a mile from Bradley Fold Junction was Radcliffe Black Lane station, just beyond the bridge in the middle of this scene. In this view, looking toward Bury, Stanier Class 8F No. **48296** (8D-Widnes) is in charge of a westbound Horbury - Garston freight on Friday July 12th 1963. Heading towards Bolton from Black Lane, which was on a level section, the gradient then climbed at 1 in 191 to a modest 1 in 340, which will take the line past Bradley Fold Junction, shortly after which a progessive two mile descent will be encountered as far as Darcy Lever on the outskirts of Bolton.   Both: *E F Bentley*

(Above) Bank Hall's Black Five No. **45041** is leaving Black Lane station behind with a featherweight load of three bogies only, on the 6.55am Liverpool Exchange to Rochdale stopping train, a 41½ mile journey lasting six minutes under two hours. At this point the line is on a level stretch whilst in about a quarter of a mile the gradient will fall progressively to Bury West (K.St), ready to negotiate the switchback of 'Bury hollow'. This detailed scene was captured on Wednesday August 26th 1964. *E F Bentley;* **(Below)** Radcliffe Black Lane viewed looking east from Ainsworth Road bridge in the summer of 1950. An unidentified 'Black Five' with a Western Division reporting number W516 (hiding the smokebox number plate) heads towards Bradley Fold Junction light engine**.** Black Lane station survived until withdrawal of passenger services between Rochdale and Bolton in October 1970 and the line between Bury Knowsley Street and Bolton (Rose Hill Junction) closed to all traffic save for a headshunt over Burnden Viaduct. *Stations U K*

(Above) Stanier class four 2-6-4 tank No. **42426** (9K-Bolton) is operating an evening westbound freight between Bury and Radcliffe Black Lane. The loco is pictured shortly before withdrawal, which took place in December of 1965;   **(Below)** For a number of years, Bolton men operated the 4/35pm Rochdale to Blackpool. This was one of the few trains not booked to call at Preston and we often arrived twelve minutes early in Blackpool Central. On weekdays, the service excluded Broadfield and ran non-stop from Bury to Bolton. The Saturday turn allowed for stops at all stations to Bolton with the exception of Bradley Fold. Here, **45078** (10B-Blackpool) is seen on the working passing the entry to Bury Gas sidings, which, by the 23rd of September 1963, when this scene was captured were out of use. The signals for Bury West box can just be observed to the left of the picture over the rear of the train. both; *Ray Farrell*

Looking towards Bury West, Bank Hall's well turned out class 2P No. **40684** catches the sun as she operates an afternoon Rochdale to Wigan Wallgate stopping train on April 8th (Wed) 1959. To the right of the engine, the playing fields of Bury Grammar School occupy the low ground between the River Irwell and the Bolton Street to Radcliffe (Central) line. The dark horizontal presence of Bury loco depot also parallels the rows of chimney pots in the right foreground. This section of line was closed to all traffic from 5th October 1970.   *Ray Farrell*

(**Below**) Bury West's bracket signals are easily visible as an Austerity operates a Mytholmroyd to Fazakerley coal train and leaves Bury Knowsley Street behind on Monday June 17th 1963. The grimy WD will face a progressive climb for the next couple of miles as far as Bradley Fold Junction with its heavy train. Much of this coal traffic was bound for the remaining loco depots of the Liverpool area, a requirement that vanished virtually overnight with the passing of steam, and providing more evidence being sought about the viability of keeping this useful east-west route open   *E F Bentley*

(Above) The 1/10pm Rochdale to Bolton makes a determined effort away from Bury in the hands of an unidentified Black Five on February 26th 1963, the year of the big freeze. Providing an all stations service between Rochdale and Bolton, the working was advertised as having a through carriage to Liverpool Exchange. The resultant connection however departed Bolton at 2.1pm with intermediate stops at Wigan Wallgate and Kirkby, the 28¾ mile journey being scheduled for forty-one minutes. To the left of the picture, an Austerity waits on the viaduct at signals ready to attack the 'switchback' of the Bury 'hollow' just before Knowsley Street station. *E F Bentley*

(Right) Just immediately west of Knowsley Street station was Bury West box. Here, Southport's Standard Class 4MT 4-6-0 No. **75016** gathers momentum as she departs with a Rochdale to Wigan Wallgate working on February 2nd 1963. Bury West box was a Lancashire & Yorkshire all-wood structure with a 28 lever frame dating from 1909. *Ray Farrell*

(Right) 42626 made Bolton its home from September 1952 until its withdrawal from traffic in October of 1965. Operating a Bolton to Rochdale service the Stanier machine now has less than a mile in readiness to attack the 1 in 85 ascent of Broadfield bank as she leaves Bury Knowsley Street behind on July 6th 1963. The route between Bury and Heywood is now of course owned and operated by the East Lancashire Railway, a remaining single line at this point having just negotiated the steeply graded 'hump', comprising embankments and a bridge to enable the preserved line to cross 'Metrolink'. The only recognisable feature remaining from this view is the Whitehead Memorial Clock Tower and no doubt makes an interesting comparison .

Ray Farrell

(Below) Almost at the foot of the climb to Broadfield lay Bury Loop Junction. On 26th August 1964, the fireman on **43913** has put a round on presumably in readiness for the climb beyond. The erstwhile 'Bury Loop', which provided a connection at Bury Loco Junction with the electrified Radcliffe line, was subsequently taken out of use on 24th March 1969. The smoking 4F must wait for the Black Five to clear the section before it can progress. Once again, the view we have here must be left to the imagination of passengers of the reinstated service to Heywood provided by the ELR. *E F Bentley*

(Right) Hughes 'Crab' 2-6-0 No. **42700** (26D/9M- Bury) now preserved, passes under Alfred Street road bridge away from Bury Loop Junction. With such a light load the Mogul will have no difficulty on the 1 in 85 climb beyond. The date of this delightful little scene is June 26th 1964. *Ray Farrell*

(Below) Unfavourable signals have checked the progress of this train of empty mineral wagons bound for the Yorkshire coalfields. The Austerities had tremendous pulling power and although by Heap Bridge Junction the gradient will have stiffened from 1 in 106 to the full impact of Broadfield 'bank', the loco will have no difficulty lifting the train up over the ensuing two or so miles. The unidentified Austerity is in typical unkempt turnout in this undated shot. The land immediately to the left of Alfred Street bridge (on the Down side of the line) had once been the site of a private siding serving the Gigg Paper mill company. *E F Bentley*

(Above) An unidentified Stanier Class 8F treads its way carefully, westwards down the final stretch of Broadfield bank and over the 'Seven Arches' viaduct which span the River Roch just west of Heap Bridge. **(Below)** A Hughes 'Crab' 2-6-0 No. **42750** (26A/9D-Newton Heath) has passed Heap Bridge Junction with the 11.47am (SO) Bolton Trinity Street to Leeds Central on its climb to Broadfield on the 4th November 1961. During weekdays, this service was purely local, calling all stations between Bolton and Rochdale. Saturdays however saw it extended to Halifax and Leeds and in doing so provided an all stations facility along the Calder Valley line (Walsden excepted as it had just closed). For some unexplained reason, an extra six minutes was allowed for the Bolton-Rochdale timings on a Saturday. These days, the embankments bordering Broadfield bank can still retain the sight and sounds of steam power, courtesy of the Bury based East Lancashire Railway. Both: ***Ray Farrell***

(Above) Just east of Heywood station lay the extensive British Railways Central Materials Depot at Castleton. As in this view dated 14th June 1962, many a long welded rail special started from here. The train is headed by the usual grimy Austerity, this particlar example being in the last month of being based at Wakefield. It would shortly transfer to Ardsley for a couple of years before a return to 56A (Wakefield) from where it was withdrawn in May 1967. The driver on **90625** has opened the regulator valve at the precise moment that the cameraman has pressed the shutter, witness the puff of steam from the anti-vacuum valve. The left hand signals on the bracket in the background allowed access to the Castleton South Fork line towards Manchester whilst the taller (central) ones took us on our way to Castleton station via Castleton East Junction. **(Below)** Ivatt Class 2MT 2-6-0 No. **46417** (26D-Bury) on Castleton pilot duty stands guard on February 5th 1958 in what was fondly known as 'Bag's Yard', an extension of the Central Materials Depot, Castleton. This loco had been allocated to Bury for just three years and would stay there until a transfer to Bolton during 1965/66. Newton Heath was its final allocation from where it was withdrawn in February 1967. Just what happened to the mounds of spent ballast seen in the foreground is not recalled. *Authors collection*

(Above) The often double headed Newcastle to Manchester (Red Bank) empty stock train is passing Castleton station and taking the main line to Manchester via Middleton Junction and Moston. The leading engine is B1 No. **61337** (50A-York), whilst Newton Heath's Black Five No. **44890** is the train engine. On a number of occasions, Bank Hall men have gone round the fork in order to turn their engine so as to be engine first back to Liverpool. On returning to Rochdale for the next part of the working, they were sometimes turned into the loop, here shown as second from the left. Seeing the signal go to clear on the right for a main line train, they forgot that they were in the loop, accelerated and promptly ran into the bridge abutment. The date of this view is July 19th 1965.   (Below) My first run on a passenger train lasted no more than about 35 minutes and it seems like only just yesterday that it took place. I can still remember smelling the new paint on 40072 after her repair at Horwich and the stiffness in the steam valves, water regulating valve and various other fittings. Here in this view at Rochdale, a B1 No. **61369** (26B-Agecroft), one of those re-allocated to the London Midland Region from the ex-GC shed at Leicester, is about to leave westbound with the 5.58pm to Manchester Victoria (all stations with the exception of Miles Platting) on August 11th 1960.   Both: *Ray Farrell*

CHAPTER SIX

TALES OF OTHER GRADES

(Right) Bolton West signal box immediately before demolition. This was the junction box where the relieving scam took place when a block inspector almost ended up working the frame himself.
N J Grundy

It is almost bordering on the uncanny when ill luck or fate seems to relentlessly pursue one individual or another. Some people just seem to be accident-prone. A signalman who had been involved in a rather serious incident during 1957, which caused his signalbox to be almost completely demolished, was removed from the signalling grade. Instead, he worked as goods shunter at Bolton's Rose Hill sidings. After a while, he was reinstated as a signalman at Moses Gate. It was a smallish box consisting of 36 levers only. At the time, there would be an early morning pilot to shunt both Up and Down sidings. In the afternoon, likewise, more shunting from about 2.00 until 4.30pm. Immediately by his signalbox door, and in front of his signalbox steps, the Up loop terminated in a stop block, literally a yard or two away. One of the regular shunting turns was visiting and a movement was taking place on that Up loop. To his horror, he saw that a small train with brake van attached was running minus the engine along the Up loop and was bound straight for his box. Just imagine the man's brain racing away, re-living the first accident. Thinking that there was a guard in the brake van, he switched the points and turned the small train out on to the Up main and away from his box. Sadly, the vehicles were running away and there was no guard in the brakevan. Off the wagons and brakevan went, running away right line. They were recovered some five miles away near Pendleton, non

the worse for wear. Railwaymen of most grades are well known to have been very good indeed about making private arrangements amongst themselves regarding relieving times. On a very regular basis, our own Running Shift Foreman on the 4/00pm turn was relieved at 11.00pm rather than the appointed 12.00midnight. So far as public transport was concerned it was much more convenient to do this at the earlier hour. Likewise, signalmen would have their own arrangements, which, strictly speaking were not supposed to happen. At Bolton's West box, for a time, such an arrangement operated. The man travelling to take up work at the box on the early turn would arrive by taxi. The signalman being relieved would then climb into the same taxi to return home. All this took place at an agreed meeting point only a few yards from the box. For a few minutes, this resulted in there being no signalman in the box. Eventually, of course, officialdom got wind of the scam and a trap was set. Even though it was very early morning, the Block Inspector turned up just as the man arriving to relieve got to the box. When asked to account for what was happening the man swung on his heel and was making for the cabin steps to leave. This then raised the official's blood pressure and he asked the 'Bobbie' where he was going. *'I'm off back home if that's how it is, so you can run the box yourself'*. Incessant pleading by the official brought the man back to his duty. As a fairly normal sort of being I

often marvelled at the ideas or theories put forward by some with whom we had to work. Some of the characters were those who carried a shunt pole or a brake stick in the various sidings we visited. The cabins where we ate our food during our 20-minute lunch break, which we were supposed to take between the third and fifth hour, were friendly places to be. Often a card game, or in some cases a game of dominos rounded off a protracted break. Many of those shunters cabins had large cast iron stoves, well stoked, often with best Yorkshire steam coal, which had 'fallen off a wagon'. On the top of the very hot stoves there resided either a large kettle or an urn with brass tap. From these appliances..............*continued on page 52*

Signalman Ken Palmer and train booker Shirley Oddie were two who worked in Bolton West box. I must add that neither was involved in the scam related in chapter six. Ken had formerly been at Lostock Junction signal box.

In the sidings at Kearsley and just by the shunters cabin where the foreman shunter used to empty the water away if it was kept boiling for too long. The sidings were at the foot of a steep incline, which led to the colliery system about two miles away. No exact date, but it is known to be after April 9th 1967. *J Ashcroft*

continued from page 51.......we brewed our tea, or for the more well off, coffee. One foreman at Kearsley made it his business to see that the water was boiling bang on brew time. If it wasn't used straight away and was kept on the boil he would throw away the boiling water in disgust saying *'they've brunt watter again'*. For quite some time the signal box at Astley Bridge Junction on the line from Bolton to Blackburn was manned by two signalmen, each sharing the work on a twelve hours basis. One of the two had become an elder statesman and with that he had become a little less adept at staying awake. The crew of an Up freight were stopped at his signal and went to the box knowing that in all probability they would find him 'out for the count'. Seeing him thus incapacitated they put the clock on a good two hours before wakening him. Naturally, he was a good deal confused but after recovering, cleared his signals and the freight carried on. Sadly for him though, he did not fully realize what had happened with the clock. He was booked for relief at 6.00am and at 6.20 by his clock was asking the station inspector where his relief was. He was of course almost two hours early. I often wonder how he explained himself out of that situation. As well as the business of manipulating relieving times there was often the chore of getting a lift home. It was quite a walk from Rose Hill Junction signal box, overlooking Burnden Park football ground, to Bullfield. The latter

was roughly adjacent to where the signal man then operating Rose Hill box lived. At just about the right time, a freight pulled in, on the fork line, to pick up traffic from Burnden sidings. As the train pulled on to the fork line, the signalman would let the locomen know that he would ride in the brake van. The men were booked for relief in Bolton station after the traffic had been collected from Burnden. Then, as the relieving set came on board, they were told that a passenger in the brake van needed dropping off at Bullfield West and please would they slow down for him to jump off? Unfortunately, on one

occasion, with the signalman having arranged to be dropped off as usual, the men were relieved at Burnden. This caused them to forget about the arrangement. The relieving men were not the usual crew but were on rest day relief and knew nothing of the passenger in the brake. A clear road was set for them through Bolton station with Bolton West's colour light at green. Diving out of the other end of Bullfield tunnels there was no way the luckless 'Bobbie' could risk jumping off. The train was next stop Preston; that day he arrived home a little late! During my short railway career, those who were a good bit higher up the ladder of promotion had to be shown at least token respect. Some of them, such as loco inspectors, still wore bowler hats, even on the footplate. The block inspector and his deputy also commanded respect. On one occasion, the official and his deputy block inspector were visiting Bradshawgate, a twenty-lever box just outside Bolton station. There, the youngish signalman immediately recognized the deputy block inspector for whom he had been a train booker and said hello, calling him by his first name. Eventually, whatever checks had to be made were completed. The two officials made to leave the box. As they approached the door, the senior of the two swung round to face the signalman. *'By the way, what's the name of the deputy block inspector?'* Came the reply, *'Gordon, oh, er, Mr.. Cremins'*. *'That's right, don't forget in future'*. With that the

Working hard after her visit to factory for general repairs, 'Austin Seven' No. **49544** gets to grips with the steeply graded incline to the colliery lines on July 29th 1955. *C B Golding*

Astley Bridge Junction signal box on the line out of Bolton to Blackburn is visible above the seventh/eighth wagon of this Brindle Heath to Carlisle freight as it crosses the Tonge viaduct. This is the box where the clock was put forward totally confusing the signalman. The engine at the head of the train in the rapidly gathering gloom is Black Five No. **45212**, which is of course now preserved. *E F Bentley*

two left the young man to contemplate. On one occasion after a training session at Bolton's Down box with some new recruits, the then block inspector returned with them to his office on what was at that time number four platform. On the official's office door, some one had chalked 'The swine of the line'! Looking at it, the official grinned and said, *'They will have their little bit of fun won't they'*? At that time his nickname was not very complimentary. On the Bolton to Manchester line, Kearsley hardly conjurs up thoughts of high-speed running or terribly important trains. With some re-signalling work having been completed prior to the closure of Moses Gate signal-box a very serious incident took place. Originally, on the approach to Kearsley 'box from the Bolton side on the Up line there had been a very tall semaphore Home signal. Eventually this was replaced with a colour light signal in advance of the box; that is to say, on the Manchester side of the cabin. In quite close proximity, a pair of slip points from the Up line to the Down sidings facilitated

such a crossing. Trains, or engines travelling on the Down line from the Manchester direction which required access to these sidings had first of all to cross to the Up line to gain entry to the sidings. Although the colour light signal provided some measure of protection for this crossover, there was now, perilously little clearance. The Kearsley signalman of the day had accepted a diesel locomotive which was travelling light engine on the Down line The man in charge of the box was a very good signalman and knew that the light engine required to enter Kearsley Sidings. The diesel carried on board a number of locomen and a footplate inspector for the purpose of route learning. He also knew that. What however he did not know was that once the diesel had crossed over from Down to Up main was that the locomotive would remain for some minutes standing there whilst the inspector pointed out the various movements and signals to those learning the route. Not knowing of, or anticipating this, indeed, expecting the engine to run straight away into Kearsley

sidings, the signalman had accepted a passenger train operated by a DMU on the Up. Obviously, with the diesel standing there he couldn't clear his signals for the DMU. Anxiously, he contacted his colleague at Moses Gate by telephone, asking the whereabouts of the passenger train, which he had offered him? The DMU was just passing Moses Gate and it was too late to stop it. There was now only one other signal before the one at Kearsley at which the drama was now taking place. The colour light at Farnworth tunnel was set at a one yellow aspect as the DMU passed it at caution with the crew-training unit still rooted to the spot at Kearsley on the same line. Eventually, the DMU arrived, head-on for, but stopping short, of the light engine. There were now two trains on the same line within yards of each other requiring to travel in opposite directions. For the luckless signalman, things now took on an unfortunate twist. The inspector, aboard the crew training loco, seeing what had happened, immediately went to the signalbox and asked to use the telephone.

(Above) This view taken on September 21st 1965 provides very good detail of what it was like at Kearsley when both railway sidings and power station were in operation. A Stanier 8F struggles with a heavy train on a gloomy Tuesday morning on towards the passenger station. On the left is the power station, coal for which was tripped into their private siding off the BR siding by electric locomotives. Occasionally, in the summer time the sidings with buffer stops accommodated excursion rolling stock. The flat roofed cabin in front of the three or four wagons served as a mess room to those whose job it was to repair wagons. Just on the fringe of the shrubs can be seen the shunters cabin where the water was teemed away if it was left too long on the boil. In the right background is Kearsley Junction Box. Still further right is the water tank used by Kearsley pilot. The Home signal to the left in the off position was moved to the other side of the box and became a colour light signal. What happened there is told in chapter six. *E F Bentley*

Speaking to control, he requested that a block inspector be contacted as a breach of signalling regulations had occurred. The block inspector from Bolton was contacted and arrived by car to relieve the signalman who he immediately suspended and sent home. An unfortunate situation had happened and concluded without any damage being done at all. The enormity of the offence though could not simply be overlooked. The man at fault had to attend an interview where he was cross-examined about the situation. When all the documentation and hearings had been concluded the man received a two-day suspension and was given a 'form one'. The incident would therefore be entered on his record of service. Occasionally, one gets into a routine at one's place of work, which is often not quite the way the rule-book tells us that things are to be done.

The fact that it was an incorrect procedure didn't seem to matter. So long as everything went all right, that was that, so to speak. One morning, strangely enough, at Kearsley Junction box again, the earlier turn signalman had just been relieved but was still present in the signalbox. The relief, having taken over the box and its operation answered the call attention from Burnden Jc. By this time, Moses Gate signalbox had closed so the section was quite a long one. Automatically he turned the commutator for the Up line to line clear, momentarily forgetting that a freight was crossing from the Up line into the Down sidings there. The earlier turn 'Bobbie' reminded the new man of the crossing movement just as Burnden offered a 3+1. *'I'll refuse it,'* said the man who was now in charge. The man off the earlier turn pointed out that as he had

turned his block to 'line clear', the train would already be entering his section. Hurriedly, Burnden Juncion was contacted and asked where the train was. A chilled feeling ran down each of the men's spine when they were told he had just passed his starters. He was therefore entering Kearsley's section. Quickly, the cabin window was flung open and frantic arm movements were made to the train crew backing across to get a move on. They were perilously short of time and some slipping on the wet track took place as more power was applied. The second the freight was inside clear, the points were reversed to lie in favour of the main line with the train almost bearing down upon them. All of us are guilty at some time of not doing things by the book. Had the commutator not been turned to the line clear block aspect, all would most certain-

Just a little way further on from the previous photograph, the signal box controlling movements within Kearsley Branch sidings. Above and to the side of the box can be seen the steps which the weary passenger had to ascend in order to gain access to the station and ticket office. On Monday March 29th 1965, Agecroft's Black Five No. **44817** is at the head of the Fisons weed killing train.   *E F Bentley*

ly have been well. As a passed cleaner, there were a couple of times when I was invited to make up the Tool Van complement. The Bolton ensemble was always kept under the cover of the shed on number six road. From the latter point there were two exits. In the event of a derailment, the unit could skirt around the blockage, provided the outlet was clear. The photograph (on page 57) will make the point clearer. Often, the fire in the galley section of the van where there was a stove to boil water and to heat food was kept lit. The unit was, therefore, ready for a quick turnout. Occasionally, lunch was taken by a few of the artisan staff in the comparative comfort of the riding section. I'm almost sure that a stock of large tins of vegetable soup were kept on board, along with a supply of tea. On receipt of a call out, a messenger would be sent to the local corner shop for milk and several loaves of thick sliced toastie bread. On one occasion around 6.30pm in the winter of 1957,the evening Blackburn to Ancoats freight suffered a de-raiment of three 'XP' vans right outside Bolton East Junction

signalbox. Ted Foster and I were asked to make up the complement of staff. Well, it was somewhat better than hanging about the shed cleaning engines! At that time, Bolton's outfit consisted only of the riding and Tool Van and one box wagon. There were a number of jacks and an apparently endless amount of wooden packing to go with the jacks to assist re-railing, and of course, metal ramps. Once into position by the side of the stricken vans the 'Tilley' lamps were lit and gear was unloaded. It was a bitterly cold night and a plum job was holding aloft the hot lamps, which helped keep hands warm. For some time we toiled in the dark cold night. Several times the de-railed vehicles were jacked up and should have fallen into place on the lines. Alas, nothing would go right. After two hours toil a halt was called to the labours whilst a much-needed break was taken. We all trooped off to the dining area in the riding van. There, Tommy Truman had prepared large bowls of piping hot vegetable soup along with stacks of toastie bread. Eagerly, we attacked the welcome nour-

ishment just as Tommy said, *'Come on chaps, 'av blown mi' nose in evry dish an 'made it nice an' salty'*. Howls of protest were heard. Tommy was one of those lively characters who always seemed to have a 'dew-drop' on the end of his nose! Often he befriended cleaners and said of his initials (TT), Tommy Trouble! Around the dawning of the twentieth century there was a growing interest in physical fitness. Already there existed movements such as the Boys Brigade, The Church Lads Brigade and a little later there followed the Scout Movement. Boys clubs were springing up and there was great interest in sporting pastimes such as wrestling. Amongst the styles of wrestling were Greek, Cornish and Cumberland. Some of the latter can still be seen at a few Cumbrian agricultural shows. A number of the wrestlers became professionals and created music hall acts. At these performances, challenges were offered to the audience to come up and have a go themselves. Around the time that a Japanese wrestler named Yoko Tani was doing the circuits, a man by the name of

We conclude our short interlude at Kearsley with a look back at the power station from a point still further along the line to Bolton just before Farnworth tunnel. A Hughes 'Crab' 2-6-0 No. **42860** operates a short freight on July 6th 1961.

D Hampson

Jack Wallwork was a guard at Bolton's Crook Street depot. Jack himself was a physical fitness expert and was also something of a champion wrestler too. Being present at a performance of Yoko's he accepted the challenge and acquitted himself very well. Indeed I have it on the authority of a close relative of Jack's that he actually defeated the champion. Needless to say from that day on he was known as "Yoko Tani". In later years when his son, who became a shunter at Crook Street, also named Jack started his railway career he was simply known as "Owd Tani" and quite naturally Jack junior was "Young Tani". After Jack's father died, Jack junior took on the nickname of "Tani".The Wallwork family of present times are no strangers to fame. "Owd Tani's grandson is the well known road walker Ron Wallwork. During the time that I was on the footplate, many of the signals were still lit by oil lamps. Naturally, these needed to be serviced periodically. Wicks, changed, or trimmed and the paraffin systems re-charged. At one particular time around the late nineteen-fifties, the semaphores at Lostock Sidings South were reported as being "out". The Block Inspector visited the scene and had a look for himself, at the same time advising the "Bobbie" that he could probably service them. But "Mr. Morgan," pleaded the signalman, "this is only a one-shift box and is closed during

darkness". He had completely overlooked the fact that the signals still had to be observed during the hours of darkness and would therefore require to be lit. Around that time, the same signalman was known as a source of some annoyance. Often he would report things of a trivial nature. A driver, reported by him for passing a signal at danger denied he had done so. Off went the chief Block Inspector to visit the man in charge of the box. An interview took place and the man was asked by how much the engine had passed the Home signal. As the driver had denied passing the peg, the matter had now reached the investigative stage. "Oh", said the man, "I went out and actually measured it, -by about this much," he indicated by spreading his arms. A look of some annoyance crossed the officials face. As he left the box, he tore up the paperwork. That was the end of the matter. Some months later the same signalman applied successfully to be upgraded, applying for the box at Rose Hill Junction. The Block Inspector advised one of the other signalmen on duty at the time that the new man would be coming to have a look. "Don't though, tell him anything "said the official, "the man thinks he knows it all". Sure enough, about an hour later. The prospective new man came wandering over the fork line just as a light engine was being run to Bolton Shed "facing road". The new man entered the box and shook hands with the

signalman on duty. The duty signalman wished him every success at the box. The new man thanked him and then said,"but there'll be no 'fly' moves". "What on earth do you mean" said the Bobbie "Oh, don't come the innocent", said the new man. "I saw that engine going on the wrong line, you can't fool me." Ah well, the facing road move was one of a number of authorized wrong line moves, but some characters were not in it when it came to the possession of intellect! Sometimes an engine was the wrong way round on shed to fulfil its diagrammed work, which might be starting from Rose Hill sidings near to Bolton East Junction. In order to save time, when ringing out, a request would be made for the engine to travel via East Junction instead of over the fork line. On arrival at East Junction, the engine could be turned into the Branch Loop wrong line, then out at the other end, clear of the points to enable it to set back into Rose Hill Sidings. The new signalman at Rose Hill signal box had not yet fully learned all the moves and refused on several occasions to accept the engine via this route. However, with some weeks having moved on, the same turn was offered to Rose Hill wrong line via the Branch Loop. The man at Rose Hill tried to refuse it but East Junction said it was on its way. At the end of the Branch Loop the engine waited with the crew impatiently blowing the whistle. Some minutes then elapsed, the driver finally deciding to walk to the signalbox to investigate. The new man was in a 'bit of a state' and didn't know how to turn the engine out of the Branch Loop, on to the main, and then reverse into Rose Hill Sidings. After a few minutes studying the diagram board the driver pulled the relevant levers and hey presto set the road for his own engine into Rose Hill sidings. As he passed the 'box and whilst backing inside he shouted to the signalman a cheery greeting. *'Let me know if you want me to reverse the points for you'.* Whilst the same signalman was working at Chew moor signal box he was responsible for causing the de-railment of an engine in the sidings there. Panic must have set in for although the main line was not affected he was all for walking off the job. At 4/20pm,the man sent the bell code 7 5 5 to boxes either side of him, signifying that he was 'switching out'. The testing block signal, 16 beats on the bell did not follow.

................*continued on page 58*

From the top of Bolton's coaling plant we can see very well the layout of the track. Starting from the left, the roads were numbered 1-12. The tool van was always kept on number 6 road from which there were two available roads to the shed outlet. Consequently, if one was blocked the alternative could be accessed.Number three road terminated outside the shed. The date here is 1st October 1957. *Colin Boocock*

During the time that I worked at Bolton MPD, Tommy Truman, here on the left of camera was in charge of catering operations on the tool van on its trips out around Bolton. He always seemed to have a 'dew drop' on the end of his nose. I was therefore always cautious about anything he had prepared. By the side of Tommy is Bart van der Leeuw, a Dutchman who lived with Tommy's family over a number of years. ***Bart van der Leeuw***

*continued from page 56.........*The Block Inspector of the day was contacted and arrived in his car to find the signalman still present. He was able to persuade the man that walking out was not the answer. During the nineteen sixties an early morning freight, 5.25am Brewery Sidings to Burnley ran via Manchester Victoria carrying perishable traffic for Bolton's warehouse. From Moses Gate, the train ran up the goods line and stopped near to Bolton East Junction. Wagons to be left at Bolton were at the front of the train. The engine now ran forward with those wagons and over the points. Once the road was set, these wagons were propelled, facing road into the Branch Loop. A special bell code existed enabling this move to be carried out. The wagons on arrival in the Branch Loop were secured and the engine re-joined its train. In order to allow the box at Rose Hill to admit Rose Hill pilot into the Branch Loop at the other end a further bell code was sent to Rose Hill signalbox. The traffic was then removed to Bolton goods warehouse. The instruction then was that Rose Hill box was to send a bell signal to Bolton East to say that the Branch Loop was now clear. With a relief signalman on duty at Rose Hill box one morning, the move just described had been completed some time before the stationmaster of the

day paid a surprise visit. The block instrument for the branch loop still showed 'Train on Line'. Asking the signalman what was in the Branch Loop the 'Bobbie' answered that there was nothing in the Branch Loop. Further asked why he had not given the authorized bell code to East Junction in order to let the signalmen there know that the Branch Loop was now clear, the man replied that there was no such code!! At Liverpool's Exchange station an inspector supervised loco movements into and out of the terminus. A very important piece of equipment there was the vacuum operated turntable. He would keenly watch when a loco had been turned to make sure that the flexible vacuum pipe which enabled us to couple up to our vacuum ejector was not left trailing on the track. If that happened, the end of the pipe would be chopped off as the loco's wheels passed over it rendering the 'table useless for weeks to come until a replacement pipe was delivered and then fitted. This caused enormous disruption to the working of trains. With the turntable out of action, locos would instead require to run light to Bank Hall shed to turn. When a quick turn around with locos working out again was required, delays would creep in. One of the inspectors was quite an accomplished beer drinker. I had forgotten about his liking for liquid nourishment when I asked him if he had enjoyed his holiday last week. Yes, he had had a good week. Where though did he go? *'To the falls'* he said. *'Which falls'*, I questioned. *'Threlfalls'* he replied laughingly.

Jack Wallwork, 'Tani' as he became known, as he was in his days as a shunter on the railway. He acquitted himself very well when invited to take on the wrestler Yoko Tani and, at his place of work was known simply as 'Tani'. ***courtesy the Wallwork family***

When Jack Wallwork's son, also named Jack started at the same depot as a shunter he was dubbed Young Tani and his father thus became Owd Tani. Of course, when Owd Tani retired, Jack, his son, simply became Tani, shown here in this un-dated portrait.
courtesy the Wallwork family

Some time between August of 1966 and May of 1967 comes this happy scene taken at Castleton near Rochdale. The engine is **78007**, a BR Standard class 2MT 2-6-0 operating the pilot. From the left are passed fireman Alan Brooks, guard Bill Corbet and shunter Eric Ashworth. Apparently, Eric would bet on most things including which of two flies would crawl to the top of a wall first.
courtesy Alan Brooks

Cliff Golding who worked at Clifton Junction as a shunter. A good deal of China clay was handled there all the way from Cornwall on behalf of Pilkington's tiles. Lead ingots also arrived at Clifton for Chloride Exide to be used in batteries. *courtesy C B Golding*

Some of the staff from Clifton Junction including the stationmaster and on the left Cliff Golding. No date for this photograph but it looks typically late nineteen fifties -early sixties. *courtesy C B Golding*

The area around Lostock Sidings South where the signalman thought that because his was a daylight only hours box he didn't need to have his signals lit. Date here is July 6th, 1954. *Authors collection*

Running light engine to shed, 'facing road' over the fork toward Burnden Junction was an often used and authorized move. The new recruit to Rose Hill Junction box though felt he knew otherwise. On April 21st 1960, trials engine No. **43139** is traveling facing road to shed. *D Hampson*

(Above-left) A special ballast is operating in the vicinity of Sough tunnel on the line to Blackburn, where a landslide has occurred on July 19th 1961. On the brake van veranda is guard Ray Camisser. *D Hampson*

(Below) Chew Moor Sidings box controlled access to and from the Metal Box factory. When a derailment occurred there, the 'Bobbie' was all for walking off the job fearing he was the culprit. With some reluctance he was persuaded by the block inspector to re-open his box and work normally. Here, Bolton's Black Five No. **45409** is operating the 5/40pm Liverpool to Bolton stopping train. *Paul Claxton*

Before the new man at Rose Hill Junction had had a chance to settle in he was sent a light engine over the Branch Loop for 'B' Side. On a number of previous occasions he had refused it. Latterly though he was unable to do so as it was already on it's way from East Junction. Waiting at the signal, and furiously whistling for the signal to be raised brought no response. So the driver went to the box to find out what the problem was. The signalman couldn't fathom out how to set the points. A few minutes study by the driver and a few levers pulled had the situation under control and as he passed the box into the sidings the driver playfully shouted he was willing to help out any time. *D Hampson*

CHAPTER SEVEN

THE ACCIDENT FILES

In one of the earliest accidents I remember, this Stanier 2-6-2 tank engine was involved in one during the early nineteen fifties. Read what happened in this chapter. *Authors collection*

The passing of signals (SPADS in modern parlance) at danger is not a new phenomenon. As I write this, there has been a good deal of speculation in the press as to why there seems to be such an upsurge of reported incidents. Years ago, when we actually had lots of signal boxes and track circuiting was not so widespread as it is today, it might have been regarded as a common occurrence. In those days if a signal was accidentally overrun we simply reversed behind the signal. If a telephone was provided at the signal the fireman got on the phone to the 'Bobbie' and the thing was squared. Failing that, if detained at the signal, the fireman went to the signal box to carry out rule 55, which relates to the protection of trains. The matter was dealt with and paperwork was avoided. Occasionally, the passing of a signal at danger might be as a result of a break in concentration. Towards the end of an eight hour shift that could quite easily happen. In preparation for relief,

the fireman might be attending to sweeping up on board and perhaps hosing down. That was quite a normal occurrence when the signals were on the driver's side and visibility good. Just such an incident under those conditions came about one Saturday evening. For a time, during 1960, I worked with Jack Byrne in the number two passenger link He was a tidy soul and I always wanted to keep the footplate spick and span too. Whilst working the 4/45pm stopper from Wigan to Bolton with three bogies only, I had almost finished my clean up on board after we had left Westhoughton. The next thing I knew was the automatic vacuum brake going on as Jack swung the drivers brake valve over sharply to the left. We lurched to a stand quickly with the dry brake blocks on our 2-6-4 tank grinding their protest. *'Whats up'* I called. *'Wi'v past 'is peg'* answered Jack. Actually, we had passed the Home signal belonging to Lostock Sidings South by about four or five yards only. Immediately, Jack bailed

out of the cab and went to the signalbox. Too late, the signalman was already on the telephone to control reporting the incident. There was no damage and there was no life in danger. Technically, one could say we were running away right line until we effected a stop. When Jack came on board with the news of what had happened I was flabbergasted. There had been no damage, no one was hurt and there would be 'paperwork' to be dealt with. Once we were given permission to proceed we finished our shift in a very subdued manner. Our booked relief was awaiting us at Bolton. We walked back to Bolton shed to sign off, quietly discussing what had happened. Back at the depot, Jack made out a report. The following week, before he could resume normal link working, Jack had to have a medical and eyesight examination in Manchester at the railway's own doctor. No medical or eyesight problems came to light. Jack therefore received a two-day suspension and a severe reprimand to be

It was a good running in turn for these class 8F locos on the bank engine at Bradshawgate. Only a minimal amount of turning what could be a stiff reversing wheel was needed. With their long firebox, fire cleaning away from depot could be a problem though. When you got one of these machines instead of an ex L&Y 'A' class, you were made up. Read about the water column incident in this chapter when one of these excellent locos was on the banker. Stanier 8F **48670** is nicely ex-works as she shunts at Chew Moor on the line to Wigan, on April 25th 1962. On that day the driver was George Smith and the fireman Tommy Withers. *Frank Dean*

(Left) A dusting of snow has fallen on March 7th 1964 on the track and surrounding rugged countryside. The branch to Hoddlesden is falling into disuse. The view looks north toward Blackburn. At this point, goods trains would be battling with a gradient of 1 in 79. Naturally, on lines such as these, catch points, or as we called them 'traps' were provided in case a wagon from a loose-coupled freight broke loose. At the traps, runaway wagons could be diverted off the track and away from the opposite running line. *H L Holland*

entered on his record of service. Occasionally, over-filling of a boiler could have alarming results. On the bank engine at Bradshawgate, with just that situation, and the safety valves lifting at full pressure a 'Crab' 2-6-0 left its short siding to bank the 8.45pm Ancoats to Carlisle fully fitted, class C freight. With the taps shut too soon, and the regulator opened just enough to carry water over to the cylinders the engine started priming. Thick cotton wool like clouds of steam billowing off the chimney top. Even though the steam brake was applied, it seemed to be ineffectual. To say they buffered up to the 'fitted' freight is to under-state the case. On this occasion, no signal was involved and luckily no damage was done. Some chaps simply were not master of the brake, be it steam or vacuum. Perhaps it's as well that in my footplate days, not many engine drivers possessed cars! There were times when one could almost say that there was a good reason why a signal was passed at danger. For many years, Bolton men had a passenger working which took them up into the hills of Bacup. It was, right up until the train was withdrawn, known simply as the Bacup. The day started pleasantly at around 8.30am.The men walking to Bolton station to relieve an earlier turn. The engine would during the years immediately after the second world war be an L&Y 2-4-2 tank and the train would be backed up in the bay

platform ready to work the 9.10am to Bacup. This train ran first of all, non-stop to Bury Bolton Street via Darcy Lever, Bradley Fold and, taking the right fork at Bradley Fold Junction, Ainsworth Road Halt. From Bury Bolton Street, the train called at all stations to Bacup. Arriving at Bacup, the engine was un-coupled and ran on to the shed there for 'loco duties'. Plenty of time was allowed for the formalities to be completed before the engine came off shed and backed on to the stock ready to work all stations to Bury where both stations would be called at. Leaving the Knowsley Street station, the train made its way via Castleton North Junction to Manchester Victoria. From Manchester, the working operated the 2.28 to Bolton calling at all stations. On the first part of the working, the morning was still and calm, it was though quite foggy. The driver, Bill Dawson had run well and with favourable signals had kept to time as far as Radcliffe North Junction where the distant signal was at caution .It would be, because it was a fixed signal. The driver knew of this arrangement, but carelessly braked a little too late. When the Home signal was sited it was on. A hefty crash on the brakes followed with the train lurching to a stand with just the engine having passed the signal. This particular signal was not track-circuited. Now for some strange reason, bearing all the foregoing in mind, the

driver told his fireman to go to the signal-box and tell the signalwoman that they had passed the peg at danger! The fireman couldn't believe what he was hearing. Most chaps would simply have been glad to have stopped reasonable, especially those operating ex-LNW locos along with their dubious tackle. The official was already on the phone to control on an un-related matter. As the fireman arrived in the box she was telling him that there was now a 'road' and had cleared the signal. Almost immediately, the fireman's story was digested and things now took on a high pitched tone. *'Did you say your driver has passed my signal at danger ?'* The fireman now tried to calm things by saying that the engine had barely put its nose past the peg. Too late, in a trice the lady was on the phone just as Bill drew up to the cabin. There was mayhem in the box with the signalwoman almost having a heart attack and the driver trying to speak to control. Eventually, Bill ended up with a form one and severe reprimand. But bear in mind the fact that the weather was foggy. During the time that I was concerned with footplate work, the nineteen-fifties onwards, we learnt our craft as we went along. There were many kind-hearted drivers who would let us drive where it was safe to do so. Things like braking distance, curves carrying speed restrictions, changes in gradient and varying types of brake were all experienced as time went on. A degree of knowledge was built up over a number of years. I don't believe there is any substitute for that. With today's policy of bringing in drivers from other backgrounds, and training them over what must be a very short period, it is no wonder that the number of 'SPADS' has increased. Lack of experience therefore must be a factor in the number of incidents reported. Some accidents, which happened to Bolton men, were of a relatively minor nature such as the de-railment of a wagon or a pair of

(Above) Viewed from the disused Hoddlesden branch, a Carlisle to Brindle Heath train is labouring up the bank with a heavy load. On this occasion, March 7th 1964, a banking engine has been taken to assist matters. *H L Holland*

engine wheels off the road. There were though some mishaps which when related send a tingle down the spine or give one an attack of goose pimples. The earliest accident I can remember taking place in the immediate vicinity concerned the 3/45pm express from Blackburn to Manchester. Looking in a westerly direction, and at the foot of Winter Hill, I could see from our Harwood home The Oaks railway station. After the station there existed an unmanned level crossing at which the gates were seldom closed. Since the road terminated short of the railway and there after only served a farm, British Railways took the view that there was no need to provide warning lights. At the time of which I write about (1951/2), the power employed on this train was one of the Stanier 2-6-2 tank engines of class 3P, or as we knew them 'Bread Vans'. One of the five engines of this class altered to carry a larger boiler, 40163, of Hellifield shed, was often used on this working Occasionally, one of Hellifields 'Crabs', either 42770 or 42784 might appear. However, with 40163 at the front of this train, which ran as an express from Darwen to Bolton, a Co-op grocery wagon was returning from a visit to the farm when it became stuck fast on the crossing just as the express arrived. The train ran into the delivery van broadside on. The wagon was swept aside as the train, travelling at some 60 miles per hour smashed it to pieces, killing its driver. Wreckage was carried almost half a mile down the track to Crompton Way bridge. The footplate crew was unharmed. After banking trains up the 1:72 to Walton's Siding on the line to Blackburn, the bank engine needed to replenish its water tank. Just beyond Bradshawgate, at Craddock Lane a water col-

umn of the parachute variety was conveniently situated on the up line. There, crews could stop before returning to Bradshawgate ready to assist the next train needing a push. When I knew him, Bill Brown was an elder statesman in the passenger link, but some years before, 1947 in fact would be on goods work. Bill was an excellent mate but the occasional lapse in concentration let him down leading to minor mishaps. On this particular occasion, the lapse in concentration could have proved fatal for the fireman. Bill and his mate had banked a train with an ex works Stanier class 8F which was "running in" at Bolton first of all on light work. On returning to Bradshawgate they needed to stop for water at Craddock Lane. Often, the reversing mechanism on such locos was stiff and so the bank engine was an ideal turn for running in because there was only a minimal amount of shunting to be done. Tender first back down the bank toward Bolton they made their water stop. The fireman screwed on the tender handbrake and the driver secured the steam brake spindle in the 'off' position. The fire man, first off the footplate, swung the heavy cast iron arm of the water column over to the tender tank. Next he climbed onto the tank top and put the leather hose into the filler hole. The on/off valve was operated by a long chain from ground level. The driver left the footplate to do just that, whilst the fireman on the tank top kept an eye on the water level in the tank. The regulator on this 8F was 'blowing through' and the driver knew of this malady. Incredibly he failed to place the engine in mid gear and neglected to open the cylinder drain cocks. Pressure in the steam chest built up to the point where the tender hand brake was overcome and the engine suddenly moved tender first. This resulted in the fire-

man becoming trapped between the cast iron water pipe and the end of the tender coal space. The fireman gave an agonizing yell as he started to feel his ribs being slowly crushed. But then, by sheer good fortune, the chain operating the valve on the water column became jammed on the tender beading. The chain, being pulled tight with the engine movement wrenched the cast iron water pipe out of its socket and it fell to the ground with a crash. After the loco had moved forward about twenty yards, the steam chest pressure had gone and the men were able to recover the situation. The fireman was sore for a number of weeks after the episode. A story was concocted between the two of them to explain the damage to the column. Those in higher office never got to know the real reason for the damage. . Fortunately, serious injury to the fireman was avoided. It would however be some weeks before the damaged arm on the water column would be put right. A run into Bolton station to top up the bank engines tank would be the likely remedy until things were back to normal. Many loose-coupled freight trains ran on the railways of this country. In order to provide safety measures in the event of a train becoming divided on an incline, or bank with those vehicles, which had become detached running backwards, catch-points were installed. In locomen's circles, these were often referred to as "traps". The steeper the bank, the more catch-points were installed. If no loose-coupled freight trains whatsoever use a particular bank, no catch points are needed. If though, loose-coupled freights use a line, which has been singled and involves a bank, then a problem arises. It's perfectly all right going up the hill, but what about coming down? When the

Blackburn to Bolton line was singled, in order to facilitate the passage of trains in either direction, electrically operated 'traps' were supplied. These could be closed for trains coming down the bank. When passenger trains were ascending the bank the 'traps' were kept open. Via a track circuit, the traps were flipped shut when the train was a short distance from the device. One early morning, a DMU was returning to Bolton with a low, but very brilliant sun shining directly on the 'traps' The drivers eyesight was particularly good and he could still read the 'bottom line' of the test card at sight tests. He wasn't perfectly sure but could almost have sworn that he saw the points 'twitch' as they were approached. As he was running through them in the trailing direction he wasn't too worried, as the worst that could happen would be damage to the point mechanism. As soon as he was able, he mentioned what he had seen to the signal and telegraph people at Bolton. The concerns of the locomen about the system were voiced at Sectional Council. Assurances were given to the effect that their fears were groundless. What though would happen if by some chance ballast were to become lodged in the mechanism? A few months after this episode, a DMU left Manchester Victoria for Blackburn at about 5/45pm. It made its booked stop at Darwen on time. A couple of train lengths after the platform, the signal stood at danger. Using the phone provided, the driver contacted the signalman and was told that trouble was being experienced with track circuits. The driver was therefore told to pass the signal at danger and go into the loop and regain the main line at the end of the loop. This would be approximately where Hoddlesden 'box had formerly stood. The signal there was also 'on'. Again, the driver was instructed to pass the signal at danger and to proceed with caution. His next signals were at the 'top points', quite near to Blackburn. As he proceeded, he next spotted the distant signal, which was showing a green aspect. Assuming that everything was now 'OK', he opened up and soon attained a good speed. Unfortunately, the distant only referred to the 'top Points' signals and the 'traps', being open, were set for a huge stack of spare rails and concrete sleepers which stubbornly stood their ground. The diescl multiple unit was wrecked. The driver survived but had two very badly shattered legs. Mercifully, because the mishap took place between Christmas and New Year, passenger loadings were light, the train usually being packed solid. Although knocked about a bit, casualties were surprisingly light. After this episode with 'traps', it was soon realised by management that no loose-coupled trains existed in the area. The catch points were therefore taken away. Tradgedy now forms the main part of our next story. At the controls of a diesel multiple unit, a Bolton driver was working the first train from Trinity Street to Kirkby on the line to Liverpool. Approaching Ince station the driver spotted something from the corner of his eye. He felt sure there was a body between the ballast and the plate girders of a bridge. Having stopped at the station, along with the guard they walked back for a closer look. The body of a young man was found with horrific injuries. The entire top of the skull was missing. All that was left was a void cavity. The brain substance was found splashed on to the bridge side. The police were called, and with a very subdued crew the train carried on with its journey to Kirkby. At first it was assumed that it was a straightforward suicide. However, at the resulting inquest, evidence was put forward which proved it to be a tragic accident. The young man had been out for the night at a local pub. Taking a short cut to his home over the railway line he had stopped to relieve himself behind the plate girders. There it was that he had been struck down by a parcels train, unknown to its crew. As the train passed he became trapped by the side of the bridge. He tried to scramble clear but had slipped on the ballast striking his head on the footboard of the first parcel van. In such circumstances, railwaymen would have simply leaned back on the bridge side and have been quite safe. Occasionally, sloppy work could lead to a disaster. Whilst it was not a major incident, there was, nevertheless the possibility of injury to those being conveyed. During steams reign, we had at Bolton a number of jobs which took us, first of all, as passenger over the Pennines to Sowerby Bridge shed. There, an engine would be prepared and we would work freight back to Bolton. Some of the work was Halifax-Burnden, Mytholmroyd-Bury, Mytholmroyd-Ramsbottom, Mytholmroyd-Royton or Mytholmroyd-Bullfield. Travel-ling 'as pass' for one of those workings, a Bolton crew were sat nice and warm in a DMU. The time was a little after lunchtime. Having left Bury, he unit was making the climb up the 1 in 85 of Broadfield bank and was approaching the 'home' signal for Heap Bridge Junction which was set at danger. In order to stop at the signal, the driver was braking and as he did so, a 'flagman' exhibited a green flag to tell the driver to pass the signal at danger. The signal was some distance from the junction points to which it related. On seeing the green flag, the driver applied power and was travelling at around 20 miles per hour as he hit the points. They were not fitting correctly and the unit became de-railed all wheels. Not only that, as the bumpy ride over the sleepers ended, the two coaches came to a stand leaning foul of the opposite running line. All this happened right by the box, so everything was stopped within seconds. Work was being carried out by the signal and telegraph department on the point rodding all of that morning. Some of the points and their rodding were un-coupled. In order to allow the safe passage of trains, a handsignalman was working under the directions of the signalman. When a train was due, the handsignalman clamped the points and called the train past the signal. After the passage of the train, the points were un-clamped with further work being carried out. When another train was signalled, the whole performance was repeated. All went well until it was time to go to lunch. Off the Signal and Telegraph men went for their dinner leaving the points clamped. After lunch, the 'S&T' men removed the clamp and started work. Regrettably, they failed to tell the signalman or the handsignalman. They then left the site to bring more materials. When the DMU arrived, the handsignalman, thinking that the points were still clamped, called the two set past the 'home' signal without checking the points, even though he had to walk past them. He didn't even see the clamp, which he had stepped over, as it was lying right in his path. No-one was hurt and the passengers were taken by foot along the adjacent Heap Bridge branch and down on to the main road where a bus was sent to take people on to Rochdale. There were many occasions when slower moving freights were run into goods or loop lines to allow faster moving passenger trains to overhaul them. On some of those occasions, drivers of the sidelined freights mistakenly took the main line signal as their own. Often the results were disastrous, sometimes spectacular. Prior to the Lancashire & Yorkshire, and The London and North Western railways having amalgamated in 1922, a serious de-railment occurred at Rochdale. The LNWR had running powers over the L&Y to Rochdale and an LNW engine was returning to Manchester light engine at the end of its working. Having been run into number one loop the driver took a clear main line signal as his own ran through the buffers and ended up in the street below. The L&Y authorities were not pleased of course. Eventually, in order to prevent such an accident happening in the future they erected a huge concrete stop block, which remained for many years. Around 1946, a Bolton crew was operating a heavy coal train out of Mytholmroyd. Unusually, they were turned into number two loop, normally only used for running round.

Aboard the 'Austin' class 7F 0-8-0 the driver stopped well clear of the stop signal. A few minutes later, the signal for number one loop went to clear and he mistakenly took it as his signal and re-started his train. At about only two or three miles per hour the engine and its train struck the concrete stop block, which didn't move. The train though did stop. The energy had to be dissipated somehow. Although the train was travelling only slowly, some of the wagons had stood on their ends, many were buffer-locked, most were de-railed and some, near the front of the train had 'squirted' sideways blocking both loops and fouling the 'Up' Main line. Both driver and fireman were off work for many weeks afterwards. The driver was never his old self again and only lived a few years after the incident. The fireman, a passed cleaner returned to work permanently as a fireman on the shunt engines at Horwich, taking no further part in main line work for

the rest of his railway career. Lastly, a very strange story. A cleaner once became fastened to a locos wheel! Whilst cleaning, a sliver of worn tyre penetrated his little finger, he was unable to move. The boiler-smith came to his rescue hearing shouts for help. The finger had to be moved to and fro until the metal broke away from the tyre leaving a big part of it in the finger protruding from each side. Under a cold water tap the sliver was pulled out. Afterwards raw iodine was administered to the wound. The treatment was as painful as the injury itself !!

(Below) Stanier Class 8F No. **48539** makes a mighty effort up the 1 in 85 of Broadfield bank towards Heap Bridge Junction. The 2-8-0 is close to the spot where the DMU was de-railed because points that had not been clamped were not fitting correctly. See story in this chapter.
Ray Farrell

CHAPTER EIGHT
SPECIALS

'Specials' created a great interest and a relief from the ordinary day-to-day trains diagrammed to Bolton Motive Power Depot. They gave one a 'buzz'. When you were marked up for a 'special', there was that sense of excited anticipation. The specials might consist of moving a permanent way engineer's train to a new location, a rake of empty passenger carriages from one-carriage sidings to another or a day excursion to the seaside. There were too, various kinds of special freight workings along with trips from Horwich Works consisting of repaired electric stock to Meols Cop, Southport, or on some occasions the units were bound for Reddish Car Shops. It is hard to say which I preferred since all of them had their good or bad points. The return of day excursions were often a problem, passengers were the worst offenders. Whilst working one of these, a Bolton crew had to stop no less than six times because of persistent misuse of the communication cord. With a train of nine corridor coaches returning to Pendleton from Blackpool the train was forty minutes late by Dobbs Brow Junction. Stopping there for what proved to be the last time, the driver identified the coach where the cord had been pulled. Earlier, an elderly lady passenger had mistakenly pulled the communication cord whilst in the toilet thinking it was the 'chain'. On this final occasion, there were several empty compartments in the side corridor coach. One had the blinds drawn. On opening its door, the driver was surprised to find a couple making love. *'What are you doing'*, exclaimed the man. *'Thee du*

thy job an' I'll du mine', quipped the driver, as he firmly crashed the doors shut. At the end of the journey, an elderly man pressed a five-pound note into the driver's hand. *'What's this for?'* said the driver. *'For not reporting us for pulling the cord in the toilet'*. came the reply. 'Derby Fours', those of the 0-6-0 variety and of class 4F were never my favorite machines on any class of work. But I'm absolutely convinced, that given the opportunity, along with the knowledge that I now have, and with a competent driver that I would fare much better than I did in 'BR' days. With their small steeply sloping firebox they needed careful firing. There was, too, an awful lot of ignorance concerning these machines where the drivers were concerned. Many said that you must not notch them up beyond a couple of turns of the reverser. That meant running with the gear set at about 45% cut off ! The trouble was, an odd one or two drivers also shoved them over into second valve with the gear thus set. I remember one occasion being in my bedroom at home. A Derby Four was on the banker and was assisting the 8/45pm Ancoats to Carlisle freight. The driver was well known as a 'flogger'. My home was over two miles away and I could here the appalling sound of the thrashing being meted out. Some chaps also said the only good 'Derby Fours' were those operating from ex-Midland sheds. It was said that they were better looked after at those depots. Now I know that was nonsense. What I didn't realize at the time was that these locos had piston valves. The old hand drivers drove them like they drove the Aspinall 'A' classes,

which operated with slide valves, two turns on the reverser and no more. Once speed was up to that which was required, the driver 'wire drew' at the regulator, steadily reducing the opening of the valve. With one of these 'Derby Four's' fresh off the works on a day excursion to Blackpool the passed cleaner was telling the passed fireman of his awful run with the return trip the day before- with another driver. By this time, the two men were walking up to Bolton station to catch the train, which would take them to Blackpool Central. The passed cleaner was so upset about the 'cold' run the day before that he threatened to go sick if the same engine was awaiting them at Blackpool's Central shed. The driver however, persuaded the passed cleaner to stick with it even if it was the same engine as the day before. Reporting their presence to the foreman at Blackpool Central shed they were told their engine number. True to form, it was the same as on the day's previous cold run. There were glum looks from the man who had the firing to do. The driver though had a plan. The first job was to obtain a dart, one of the set of fire irons. Next, the six-foot implement was shoved under a convenient rail then heaved upward so that it was bent, almost at right angle. Hoisting it up on to the footplate, the business end was stuck in the firebox and a huge piece of clinker moved from its resting-place right under the door. No wonder steaming had been a problem. The concrete-like block was unceremoniously dumped overboard. Under the directions of the driver, the fireman built up the fire beneath the door and was told very firmly

As late as 1957, Blackpool Central shed, pictured here, received a new roof of a steel framed variety. Little did BR know at that time that by the end of 1964 the shed would be closed. A mixed bag of diesel electrics and Stanier machines on view on June 3rd 1963. From left to right, **45574** *India* (24E-Blackpool)- **42625** (24E-Blackpool) - **46165** *The Ranger (12th London Regiment);* (5A-Crewe) - **D13** - **46166** *London Rifle Brigade* (12B-Carlisle Upperby) - **45236** (12B-Carlisle Upperby) - **D302.**   *Peter Fitton*

that no coal was to be put at the far end. Once they got under way, the fireman was positively beaming as they went over the flying junction on the Marton line at the correct speed and with the boiler bursting at the safety valves. With the gear notched up toward middle and the regulator over in the quadrant block they were playing with the job and arrived at Bolton a minute in front of schedule. Proof indeed of the capabilities of these much-maligned goods engines. How I wish I had made a note of the event of one of my more unusual runs. Together, George Monaghan and I walked to Bolton station one morning at 11.00am to relieve a special. The year was around 1958. The train eased to a stand soon after our arrival at Bolton and was bound for Aintree. The power was nothing out of the ordinary, an Austerity belonging to Bury (26D) No. 90205. The train, strikingly, consisted of 37 conflats on which were loaded the same number of bright red Massey Ferguson tractors, all for export. With so light a train we were at our destination within the hour and I think that day George was in a hurry to get there as we fairly sped along at the sort of speed which made these W.D. locomotives uncomfortable to ride on. This was one of the few occasions when I worked a fully vacuum fitted freight with one of these

locomotives. After leaving the engine at Aintree shed, we travelled back to Bolton shed 'as pass'. As so often happened on these sorts of jobs, we finished the day kicking our heels in the drivers lobby awaiting fresh instructions. I had booked on at 10.00am, but George would have to stick around much longer as he had started his day at 11.00am. It wasn't very often that you went working on loan as a fireman at another depot. What was even more remote was doing that on your rest day. Even worse, when one's rest day was a Saturday. Looking back to that time of around forty years ago I am amazed that I worked rest days. I was single, and the tax man took such a big slice of the pay. I'm afraid I was a pain in the neck at that time so far as the Running foreman was concerned. Sometimes I would work rest days, other times I was a bit stubborn about it and would not. However, John O'Neil and I signed on at 6.47am during the summer of 1963 to travel to Blackpool on the 7.19 from Bolton. Blackpool was very short of men, and there were two jobs to cover. As one was a 'Special' to Nottingham and the other one was the passenger pilot at Central station, it was decided we would toss for who went on the 'mainliner'. I shouted correctly, but whether or not I won was debatable, as we will see. Arriving in the drivers lobby to

report to the foreman, I was introduced to Bill Fisher, a Blackpool man who would be my mate for the day. The engine was prepared and was standing under the cover of the shed. A Hughes 'Crab' 2-6-0 looking decidedly dirty, and as we were to find out, she was not in the best of condition. Trying the exhaust injector in order to swill down aboard the footplate I saw that most of the water was just running away at the overflow by the engine footsteps. Regulating its flow by means of the handle beneath the window was of little benefit, as half of the flow was simply going to waste. The live steam injector was tried and worked, after a fashion. We could hardly set off with just one injector working so fitters were summoned. After about twenty minutes, some improvement was effected but there was still a dribble on to the floor. We took a decision to trust that the feed would remain functional, but would it? Leaving Blackpool's Central station we were in apple pie order and, after negotiating the curves of Blackpool South, stormed up the bank to Watson Lane Bridge, and on more level track we bowled along toward Bradkirk. On went the exhaust injector, or rather it should have done. We were back to square one; more water was going on the floor rather than in the boiler. We floundered along. Trying to operate the

Better times here for Blackpool driver Bill Fisher aboard Royal Scot Class 4-6-0 No. **46146** *The Rifle Brigade* at Euston on the London to Blackpool service. No date for this scene but a far cry from the Nottingham special with a lend out 'Crab' and two dodgy injectors. *Dave Dunstan*

exhaust injector was futile. The live steam one was brought into play, its song was of a sickly note! Our route took us over the North Union south of Preston and on to the Whelley Line at Standish Junction. Then, over a piece of railway over which we as Bolton men, only operated freight, the line down past De Trafford Junction where we collected a conductor driver from Springs Branch shed. From there, we rolled on over the switchback railway where colliery subsidence manifested itself, on towards Bamfurlong but swinging off sharply left at Amberswood East Junction on to the Great Central line running via Hindley South, Bickershaw & Abram, Culcheth, and Lowton St Mary. There, tall weeds were invading the track, foretelling of impending closure. By the time we arrived at Cheadle Heath, we were mighty glad to step off to be relieved by Heaton Mersey men. Newton Heath (26A) occasionally had a shortage of footplate crew and was unable to cover all the work, usually in the summertime. Local holiday times, or 'Wakes Weeks' were really busy periods. A good many 'specials' were laid on to cater for increased passenger numbers. I have heard it said at such times that you would be nodding to your neighbour at 7.30 in the morning as you locked up the back gate at home. The next time you greeted each other was about noon 'on the prom' at Blackpool. In

Lancashire, amongst the cotton towns to take their annual holidays in the nineteen fifties and sixties were Oldham and Rochdale in mid June. At the start of one of those periods, two Bolton crews were dispatched to Newton Heath shed to work a special to Blackpool. One engine would work the train throughout whilst the other would assist over the heavily graded line from Dean Lane up via Failsworth and on to Oldham and Rochdale. At the latter station the assistant engine would uncouple and quickly run light engine to Bolton shed for servicing. There were long faces from most of the four when they were given two 'Derby Four's'. Now the two chaps on the assisting engine were of the very 'short fused' variety. As they prepared their engine, the other crew on the same road could hear raised voices and some choice language too. Before long, the fireman of the assisting loco could be heard piling a huge load of coal in the firebox. It was a very warm morning and before too long the fireman was running in a sweat. Within a short space of time smoke was pouring off the chimney top and the engine was blowing off furiously. Other drivers were complaining about the noise and smoke. It didn't take long before the R.S.F. came out of his office to see what was going on. After he had said his 'two-pennarth' to the crew, the two men aboard the 0-6-0 could be heard

shouting and cursing at each other at the tops of their voices. Those on the train engine, where the fireman, a passed cleaner, obtained a bent dart, shifted the customary 'gravestone' from under the firedoor and chucked it overboard. After that, he built up the fire under the door, having been restrained by the driver from putting on a 'boxful'. An hour and a half was allowed for preparation and coupling together, 'bags' of time. At the appointed time the two locos crossed into Lightbowne carriage sidings and coupled to nine bogies. Eventually, the train drew into Dean Lane station where a platform full of trippers piled into the empty compartments. At the signal from the guard they set off with an almighty wheelslip from the leading engine. After only a short distance, its driver signalled that he was running short of steam and water in the boiler. Far too much coal had gone into the firebox, hampering good combustion and preventing good steaming. At the next stop, Failsworth, the train engine driver went forward to tell the driver of the assisting 4F that they were doing fine and would he just simply give them a good start from each of the successive re-starts. Would he then just put on a breath of steam, enough to move his own engine? That day, the driver of the train engine who was not one to 'thrash' an engine certainly did so. Full regulator and with not much notching up, the 0-6-0 did everything expected of it. It lifted the nine coaches on that bank mostly on its own. At times, both injectors were used mostly when the regulator was closed, steaming was good. By the time the train had arrived at Rochdale, after the easily graded stretch from Royton, the engine at the front had recovered the situation and was now blowing off again. With voices still raised, and the safety valves fit to burst, the leading loco uncoupled and ran light to Bolton shed where they would have the unpleasant task of paddling out all that live fire. There was no doubt that time had been lost, but 'specials' were very easily timed and with an engine steaming so well there was no difficulty in regaining the time lost before arriving at Blackpool Central. For day excursions from Bolton, Southport was a popular destination during the late forties and the nineteen fifties. Often, queues for such trains would

Part of our journey to Cheadle Heath, where we were relieved, took us over the Whelley line and on to the former Great Central route at Amberswood East Junction (from the right in this picture). In this view, Fairburn tank No. **42113** (9E-Trafford Park) is operating the 09.00 Wigan Central to Manchester Central all stations service on Saturday July 6th, 1963 as it enters Hindley South. The Wigan Central line saw its passenger service withdrawn on 2nd November 1964. The Amberswood East Jcn - Hindley South connection closed to all traffic from 22nd February 1965, bringing an end to the facility enabling access to the GC route and through running described in the chapter.
E F Bentley

stretch from the booking hall at Trinity Street station well around the corner and down Station Street. Often, the only 'berth' on some trains was the guards van. On hot summer days, the smell from the empty fish boxes piled up therein, mingling with the ladies *Outdoor Girl*, or *Evening in Paris* perfume was some experience! Occasionally, on Sundays, with men being paid at the rate of time-and-three quarters, the men operating a special would be required to work the excursion both ways. Booking on duty at around 7.30 or 8.00am they would operate the train to its destination, where the carriages would be shunted into their siding for cleaning and servicing. The engine and men would then take the engine to the shed, clean the fire, top up the tank, and do whatever servicing was required. After that, the crew 'booked off duty' and took their meal break. They were then free to stroll around the resort or do whatever they fancied. Such workings were known as 'Short Rests'. At a prescribed time, they booked back on duty ready to operate the train back home. The main idea was

that it saved a set of men signing on to bring the train back. It was thus a less expensive way of operating the excursion. It was vitally important to take enough food to last the day. One fireman operating such a turn was told, the day before the excursion, by the driver he would be working with not to bring any food, just something to make a brew with. The man couldn't begin to imagine what was planned but, nevertheless, complied with the instruction. As was often the case, a works engine 'Crab' 2-6-0 was power for the job and there were no problems, with the train running to time. After loco duties had been done on Southport shed and the engine 'bedded down' the men spruced themselves up and went for their dinner. The driver's plan, which he had applied successfully several times, was put into action. A fish and chip dinner was on the agenda and a suitable venue was sought. After strolling around the town centre for a little while, a chippy was found which appealed to them. The time for 'action' had arrived. Walking into the shop, the driver went straight to the owner and

suggested that as they were on duty, and therefore in dirty working overalls, could they have a table out of site of regular customers so as not to discourage trade. The owner obliged by putting up a table in the back of the shop away from the main area and brought them two huge platefuls of fish, chips and peas along with two steaming mugs of tea. At the end of the meal the owner came to see if everything was in order. As expected, it was. How much though did the men owe the proprietor? *'Nothing'*, came the reply. *'We should be jolly grateful to chaps like you giving up your Sunday and bringing us trade into the town'*. As expected, the stunt had worked again! These jobs were always highly prized. Even though we booked off duty whilst awaiting the return working we were paid throughout. The rate was time and three quarters. Around 1958, an Accrington 'Black Five' would be spare on Bolton shed. The 4-6-0 would have worked into Bolton on Colne-Burnden freight. The engine arrived on Bolton shed around 3.00am. It was then re-prepared to operate the 6.42am freight

A selection of handbills containing programmes for additional train services/excursions from the year's 1959/60 &1963

to Horwich works. Loadings were just about within a Class Five's capability. After the train had been propelled on to the works via 'Station Line' a run, tender first propelling a brake van to Westhoughton followed. The route was via Horwich Fork Junction, Hilton House, Hindley and Blackrod Branch Junction, and Crow Nest Junction where reversal took place. The small train then ran on to Westhoughton goods yard. A warehouse operated there and a good deal of coal traffic existed. Indeed, up until the opening of the Healey Mills facility, empty coal wagon trains ran from there to Bradley Wood in Yorkshire. Eventually, after some shunting, a train was made up for Halliwell. The engine finishing its turn by arriving on shed at Bolton for about 1/00pm. After more preparation, the engine operated the 5/18pm stopper to Accrington often with a stores van for Accrington shed. Return to Bolton was by double heading Colne-Stockport parcels. For a short time, this engine was required to bank Brindle Heath to Carlisle before being relieved by Bolton men to work the 11/40pm Bolton to Colne freight. So the most was made out of the 'visitor' As there was no working for it on a Saturday

or Sunday it was spare on Bolton shed. During the local Blackburn holiday period of July 1958 I had the good fortune to be marked with 'Slinger' Wood on a short rest special to Morecambe via Blackburn and Hellifield. We started our day at 8.00am. The power was the spare Accrington 'Black Five' No. 44692. After making sure everything was in order on board we ran tender first to Moses Gate to back on to our stock, nine bogies. At this distance in time I am fairly sure they were not corridor stock. They were, in all probability the coaches kept there for operating the Royal Ordnance Factory (ROF) service to Euxton, which was not required Saturday or Sunday. Running empty stock up the bank our first stop was made at Darwen. I believe that we then only called at Blackburn before arrival at Hellifield for water. We had a load of coal bricks to use first. Obviously the engine had been coaled up under the hopper intended for freight engines. No thought had been given to the fact that the engine would be used for passenger traffic on the Sunday. It was a hot sticky day; dust from the coal bricks was swirling around in the cab. The bitumen used in the process of forming the briquettes was shocking stuff.

It found its way onto one's face and, more painfully into the eyes causing a burning sensation. Some of the rubbish was shovelled off whilst we topped up our tank in order to be rid of it. By the time we arrived at Morecambe Promenade station our eyes were red raw. After putting away our empty carriages we dealt with the fire and turned the engine ready to operate the return working. The boiler was filled up and the steam pressure allowed to drop to around 75lbs per square inch. The fire was made up under the door. We could now have a wash in the messroom facility provided and have our food and a much needed brew. Overalls removed and after a wash and brush up we made straight for the St John Ambulance Brigade post on the Prom. There, our badly affected eyes were treated with a liquid substance to help quell the burning sensation. A note was made in their accident book. That evening on the return journey, which was 9/15pm from Morecambe Promenade, 'Slinger' was determined he wasn't going to have the same eye problem again. Against rules he wore his glasses as a protection against the deadly dust for most of the journey home.

Hindley South once again, but this time from the opposite side to that shown on page 69. As mentioned previously, this useful cross-country route as far as the Cheshire Lines at Glazebrook, was deemed uneconomic and closed to through traffic early in 1965 to a point just north of Lowton. Here we see Stanier Class 4 tank No. **42647** (8F-Springs Branch), leaving Hindley South with the 13.10 (SO) Manchester Central to Wigan Central train on October 10th 1964, traversing a short part of the route taken by the Blackpool-Nottingham trains on which the author worked as far as Cheadle Heath. The service from Manchester Central to Wigan Central was withdrawn from 2nd November 1964, some three weks after this photograph was taken. Prior to October 1952, Hindley South had been known as Hindley & Platt Bridge, a name it held for sixty years after a renaming in 1892 from the original short lived Strangeways & Hindley title. The spoil tips in the background screen the town of Hindley from view.   *E F Bentley*

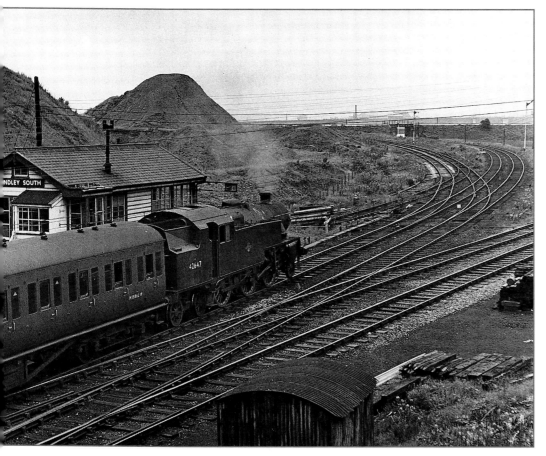

(Left) A superbly clear shot of Hindley South with **42647**(8F) operating a Manchester Central to Wigan Central service (25th July 1964). For a brief period between October 1963 and April 1964, this loco worked out of Wigan L&Y depot. For the next two years it was allocated to Springs Branch from presumably where it was diagrammed to work the service seen here. Few passenger trains off the Wigan Central line were scheduled to cross here with the exception of the 2.6pm to Manchester and 2.2pm to Wigan on Saturdays. The train, the 14.03(SO) to Wigan Central, is cleared to take the route which passes through the bridge opening in the middle distance. The lines to the left provided connections with the Whelley line at Amberswood West Junction and subsequent links with the North Union (WCML) and Lancashire Union routes south of Wigan. The lines to the right served the connection with Amberswood East Junction and the route of the *Bolton Engineman*. The many colliery waste tips like the two pictured, characterised the area around here. Most of these extremely useful chord lines had been dispensed with by the end of the 1960's although the Whelley line soldiered on until 1973.   *E F Bentley*

Bolton Trinity Street, 7th March 1962. Queues for special trains to Blackpool or Southport often stretched out of the station building and well down Station Street. Unfortunately, the full effect of the red Accrington brick frontage of 1903 was somewhat diminished by the iron canopy built in front of it. A full appreciation of the frontal features was hidden from general view until May 1968 when the covered approach was removed in readiness for the reconstruction of Trinity Street bridge. The whole building was subsequently removed as a result of deteriorating steelwork supporting the station building and a new entrance, which included the clock tower, resited in Newport Street. Station Street is to the right. *Authors collection*

(Below) Station Street where the queues for day trips often wended their way. Hardly anyone around though on a dismal March 7th 1962. Posters on the station buildings tell us that the day trip fares, by diesel train no less, to Blackpool, were six shillings and three pence (about 33p in today's terms) and five shillings and six pence the day after. Why the difference? No 25 bus for Halliwell waits for business. *Authors collection*

Burnden Sidings, on the left of this view, lay beyond the angle created by the fork line off the Manchester to Bolton line and the route to Bury. The latter lines are those curving in from the left, and the line to Manchester itself straight ahead. On that very line to Manchester, Black Five No. **45048** has just passed Bolton East Junction with the 8.25am Glasgow and Edinburgh to Manchester Victoria at 12.45pm on Thursday November 16th 1967. Walker's tannery is the large building to the right of camera. The sidings in the shadow of the tannery were locally referred to as 'A' Side where the loaded parcel vans were stored. *E F Bentley*

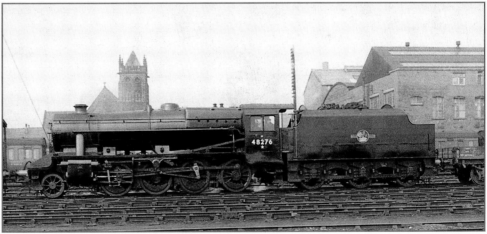

(Centre) Standing at the Moses Gate end of Burnden Sidings is a balanced Stanier Class 8F No. **48276**. The star on the cab side beneath the number indicates the fact that the engine's wheel set is balanced. The loco is ex-Horwich Works, and judging by the re-paint, heavy repairs have been undertaken. In the right background we again see Walkers tannery whilst the steeple of the long disappeared St Bartholomew's Church peers over the 2-8-0s boiler. The date is June 4th 1958. *D Hampson*

(Right-lower) Looking from a similar spot to the previous photograph, but viewing more toward Burnden Junction signal box, which is just visible, Stanier tank No. **42547** ambles past on the Up Main with the 8.19am departure from Trinity Street bound for Manchester Victoria. Note the gunpowder wagon in the right foreground on May 20th 1960. *D Hampson*

(Right-upper) When I was in the disposal link in the summer of 1959 there were few oddities to report. There was one of course when this J39 class arrived in the early hours of July 31st of that year. **64748** (9G) had worked in on Halifax to Burnden on one of the rare days that I had a camera at my disposal. The time is around 6.00am luckily the sky was bright, so it was possible to get this shot. *Author*

(Right) Also on the 31st July 1959, passed cleaner Derek Jones has a weeks work as steamriser. Here he is taking a breather after building up the fire on 64748 on number 12 road at Bolton shed. *Author*

(Left) An unusually clean Austerity treads carefully down Miles Platting bank with a mixed freight on April 2nd 1960. The WD 2-8-0 No. **90088** is almost level with the platform ramp and in a few yards the train will be stopped to lift up the brakes pinned down by the crew in order to descend the bank safely. The new Manchester Victoria East Junction signal box is under construction on the left of the WDs smokebox.
Frank Dean

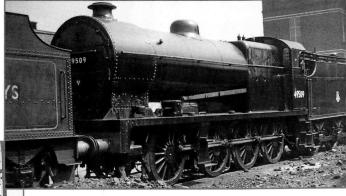

(Above) Ex works 'Austin Seven' is stabled near to the buffers at the Beehive Mill end of the shed yard where a large coal stack once existed. **49509** (26F) is obviously ex works during April/May of 1953. *M J Blackburn*

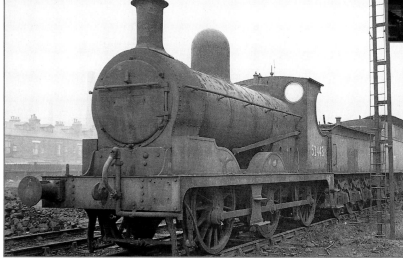

(Left) This withdrawn 'A' class 0-6-0 No. **52443** occupies a position more or less where the coal stack was formerly sighted. There is still a small amount of coal stacked up, but nothing compared with earlier days. This maid of all work has seen the end of its working life on February 18th 1961 and waits scrapping. *Paul Claxton*

At the time when many locomen were at work, most folks were in their beds fast asleep. During the nineteen fifties, when I was on my way to work I seldom saw anyone save for the odd policemen in Bolton town centre after midnight. Those days are so far removed from the 'live' town centres of today and it is almost impossible to imagine what it was like. Many of the roads had half of their lights switched off at midnight. Some roads became completely unlit after the 'witching' hour. Out in the fields of Harwood, I occasionally took my dog for a late night or early morning walk. Living as I then did opposite the Bolton to Blackburn line and at a distance of about two miles, I could clearly hear, born on the westerly wind, freight trains descending the 1 in 72 bank, their side rods clanking a rhythmical message as they made their way down the gradient. Occasionally, the clanking would cease briefly as the 'Black Five' at the front of the train 'picked its wheels up' in an uncontrolled slide, the brake having been over applied. The driver would then

regain control and the clanking would be audible once more. I recall hearing such a sequence for quite some distance until speed had been brought down to an acceptable level. One evening, at almost midnight, the 11/40pm Bolton to Colne, with just under a bank engine load, slipped itself to a stand just up the bank out of Bolton at the point where Crompton Way passes under the railway. The engine was an Accrington 'Black Five'. With their six-foot driving wheels and a greasy rail this often happened. In order to try to re-start, the driver made the mistake of letting part of the train run back in order to gain some impetus. Regrettably, he either forgot that there were catch points in the vicinity, or simply misjudged their position. Several wagons were de-railed on to their sides. Some residents found their back gardens full of coal next day. Doubtless some of it found a way into adjacent coalsheds! During the 'small hours' it was not usual to use the Tannoy announcing system on Bolton station's platforms when requiring to call someone. If for instance the wagon 'tapper' was

needed to look at a suspect vehicle on a train, the Tannoy was turned on and the announcer simply blew air into the 'mike' several times. Then, very softly, he would say, *'Tapper, tapper, cum on tapper'.* Eventually, the noise awoke the man in the carriage and wagon department room on the platform. With carbide lamp in one hand and hammer in the other it wouldn't be long before he arrived on the scene. It was not immediately obvious that there was a railway police presence at Bolton. When the official was required on the platform it was usually announced by one of the platform inspectors. *'Two seven, two seven, report to the Up side inspector'.* There were of course occasions when his help was needed. By the nineteen sixties, Bolton had a large amount of mail order parcels to deal with. Towards the end of steam, some loaded wagons were stabled in 'A' side parallel with Walkers Tannery. During a quiet spell at around 2.00am, at Burnden sidings just opposite 'A' side, a brew was being taken by those whose job it was to marshall wagons in the sidings. The driver heard a commotion

Farington Junction, further south along the main line from Preston, near to where the incident involving the two passed cleaners took place. The coaling plant of Lostock Hall shed is visible in the right background. On May 25th 1967, Black Five No. **45280** is at the head of a southbound freight. *N Fields*

just outside the shunters hut and went to investigate. Almost immediately, he was practically bowled over by someone running at full tilt. Realizing that the person was of somewhat smaller proportions than himself, the driver clung onto the fleeing person. Incessant pleading to be let go followed. It was now obvious that it was a youngster who now begged to be let go as he was only taking a short cut and didn't know he was doing wrong. Lights now appeared from others on foot across the main line. They were the company police and were about to give chase. An approaching mail train bore down preventing them. The driver hung on to his assailant. When the officials arrived with the driver and his charge it became apparent that he and his father were old 'customers'. He was therefore taken away for questioning. As I have previously written, over the years we had, at Bolton, a number of freight turns which took us first of all 'as pass' down the Calder Valley line to Sowerby Bridge shed. Depending on what we were doing afterwards, the engine might have been prepared for us. If it was a straightforward working, say from Mytholmroyd to Bolton we might be required to prepare the loco ourselves. For a number of years we also had a turn where we first of all went 'as pass' to Low Moor shed and collected either an Austerity or a Stanier 8F. For a period around 1960 whilst I was on disposal duties, this very working brought on shed a J39 0-6-0, from the Eastern Region, often from Gorton shed (39A). These locos had a drop grate which was operated via a screw handle on the footplate. However, returning to the freight working. For some time, we ran first of all light engine to Low Moor sidings and operated a small number of 'fitted' vans to Halifax where more traffic was attached. From there we next called in at Mytholmroyd where a full train was made up. Next stop would be Rochdale mostly to put off vehicles. Then, on mostly easy graded track we were next stop Bolton (Burnden Sidings). This turn paid very well, often eleven or twelve hours were made. If that happened all five nights, the next week's pay packet was swelled to handsome proportions. There was very little car traffic about on the roads and around 12.30am with a train

ready to leave Halifax the surrounding hills were particularly black with road lights switched out all around. On this occasion, the guard was a well known joker and winking at the driver, decided he would have a little fun at the fireman's expense. Looking up into the hills, a row of lights could be seen gradually descending. It was in fact the last bus returning to town. The fireman, not the brightest of souls, noticed the lights coming down with apparently no sound. The guard, persuing his twisted sense of humour, persuaded the fireman that, since there was no noise, the engines on an aeroplane had failed and that it was about to crash. A minute or two later, both guard and driver realized that the fireman was no longer present and that they were due away. Persistent shouting for the fireman failed to bring him back to the footplate. Some minutes elapsed and he finally returned, having been to the signal box to report to 'Control' that a plane was about to crash and would they summon the police please. There was a great 'hullabaloo' at the local police station. By the time that the guard had been on the phone to say that it was a prank that had badly mis-fired, the train was seriously delayed. Subsequently, as on such occasions, much paperwork was flying about for weeks after the event,

as someone had to be blamed for the resultant delay. During the hours of darkness, the shed seemed to take on a quieter sort of routine. There was never the activity that took place during the hours from, say 8.00am to 4/00pm. There were no shed staff such as sweepers, nor was there anyone working on the ash pit until midnight. The coal hopper attendant would have gone home by 5/00pm and only a few fitters and their mates remained on duty. If, like me, when I was sixteen you and an engine cleaner, there wasn't the same supervision. I always felt that the place had an informal and relaxed air. Even the shed master went home at 5/00pm, so we weren't under his watchful eye! Just occasionally, whilst driving to work, one might be surprised to be 'flagged down' by someone needing a lift. At 3.00am I was motorcycling to work along Newport Street toward Trinity Street when such an occurrence took place. The youngish chap looked quite normal. I was though, amazed when he asked me if I knew where he could buy a pair of clogs! I gave him a lift to the sheds and suggested he ask our stores issuer who could 'procure' most things for a suitable fee! The Motive Power Depot was a great place for the local Bobbie to spend an hour or so in the small hours and

When these BR Standard 2-6-0s were brought into service, it was 'decided' by higher authority that as they only had six oiling points each side, one oil bottle with spout would suffice. See chapter 10 to read about the pandemonium it caused amongst the 'old hands'. A Standard class 4MT 2-6-0 No. **76035** has been outshopped at Horwich in March of 1958 and is almost ready to leave for trialing at Bolton.   *J Davenport*

chat over a cup of tea to the RSF. Just how pleased the foreman would be at having his attention diverted I'm not really sure, as there were lots happening in a quieter way. There was paperwork to be dealt with and logbooks to be completed. One of the logs kept was day-to-day information such as the state of the weather, numbers of men off work, engines on the books and so forth. Some of the comments could be quite funny or somewhat subtle. One of the firemen at the shed was a very good artist at the keys of either electronic organ or piano. On one occasion in the middle of the night, the book records that this man's wife rang the shed to say her husband was reporting sick for an early morning turn. The information was duly recorded with the added comment 'loud piano playing heard in background'. Men from both passenger and goods links would be signing on. Many of them preparing locos, some of them complaining bitterly when they had an engine known to be in poor condition. Fitters to be attended to, chaps signing off and the 11/00pm disposal men having been inactive until around 2.00am shedding engines would command his time. At Bolton, during the years I was a footplateman, there was a 10/00pm disposal set and one at 11/0 as well. It was always 'generally agreed', that the first seven locos arriving on the ash pit for disposal would be dealt with by the 10/00pm men. Thus, by getting a move on, they could have their quota in by 1.30am and be on their way home by 2/00am. The only difficulty was you went home with a sweat on. In those days there were no showers at home, just the tin bath, so a sponge down at the sink had to suffice. On our smallholding we were on well water. The single brass tap over the sink delivered cold water only. In the summer time it was reduced to a drip. In order to fill a kettle under those conditions, the bowl in the sink was turned upside down. The kettle was then placed on the upturned bowl and allowed to fill at its own speed. Towards the end of steam we had several jobs, which operated quite heavy trains out of Ashton Moss Sidings to other destinations in or around the Manchester area such as

Brewery, Chadderton Power Station, or Brindle Heath. Very early one morning, at dead of night, a very heavy train operated by a 'Crab' 2-6-0 was gently making its way around the curves of Miles Platting toward the top of the bank. Next to the engine there was one vacuum fitted wagon. But with so heavy a train, it was hardly much use as a braking force. The driver was taking a turn on the shovel and was allowing his experienced passed fireman to drive, fully expecting him to stop at the top of the steep incline which lead to Manchester's Victoria Station in order to pin down brakes. Instead, he allowed the train on to the bank. The immediate result was that this heavy train bound for Brindle Heath started to run away, completely out of control. In a panic, the passed fireman flew to the whistle in order to give the dreaded series of short 'pop' whistles denoting train running away. The driver though prevented him from doing this as the signals in front were showing green and as long as they were coming 'off' they would get away with it. Because it was very early morning and there was little traffic about they were lucky and were routed via the through road, but still went through Victoria Station like the Liverpool 'Flyers'. They were well on the way to Salford before the train was properly under control again. All the way whilst running out of control, the driver couldn't help thinking about what happened when a petrol train ran away down the same bank in the nineteen forties and which made such a mess of Victoria Station. Looking back, it is amazing that the passed fireman on the 'Crab' actually thought that the one broke

mineral wagon plus the engines own brake would be enough to hold them on the steep bank. It was just one of many 'scrapes' he got into. At dead of night, fateful things can happen, and at times because of something we have done we feel guilt because of the nature of the circumstances. During the later mid morning period at Bolton shed, one of the senior passed firemen had signed off duty and was ready to go home, having been on an early morning turn. For several days, he had been having trouble kick-starting his 250cc motorcycle. This particular morning was no different so far as the bike was concerned. It simply would not kick-start. When a colleague arrived he was fair worn out trying to 'bump' start it. The new player in the drama now insisted on looking at the points. They were grossly out of alignment and needed re-setting. Next, the spark plug was examined. Not only was it badly carboned but also was the wrong size. The colleague was on his motorbike and against much protest insisted on going to the dealers for a new plug. When fitted, the motorcycle started at the first kick of the lever. It was a miracle that the bike had ever run in such a state, but now, full of thanks he sped off home happily. The following day, very early, at dead of night, whilst riding his motorcycle to work for the same turn, he was run into and killed on the spot by a drunken lout. When he heard the news, the man who had been the 'Good Samaritan' now felt very bad indeed. If only he had not helped to mend the bike, perhaps the man would have been later and thus the accident would have been avoided. If only! In the years after the Second World War, food

(Left) Another shot of the concrete building, formerly a firelighter store but yet another exmaple of one of the many 'standard' concrete products emanating from the Newton Heath workshops. A light dusting of snow has fallen around an out of service **42626**, which failed a boiler examination on October 15th 1965. She was withdrawn a few days later on October 23rd. Supplied as a new engine to Bolton on August 5th 1938, 42626 went to Newton Heath shed on 21/1/39. The engine was transferred back to Bolton on 20th September 1952 where it remained until withdrawal.   *S A Leyland*

items were in short supply and still rationed. I remember asking my mother on a number of occasions at the local shop if I could have some sweets. More often than not I was given a firm no, with the added assertion that in any case, we didn't have enough coupons left in our current ration book. It was though often the case that certain items could be procured if one was 'in the know'. One very dark moonless night a freight was preparing to leave Bolton. As was customary, the guard came up to the footplate to let the driver know the load and number of vehicles attached. Instead of staying aboard the engine, the driver was on the floor and together the two men talked in low tones. The fireman was conscious that somehow he figured in the conversation as sideways glances and nods were exchanged twixt guard and driver. Presently, the driver climbed up on to the footplate. Looking his fireman in the eye, the driver told him that at a certain point he must close the engine's damper and let steam pressure fall back, as they would be stopping and on no account must the engine be allowed to blow off. On reaching the pre-determined spot, the driver left the footplate and walked back down the train. A few minutes later he returned with his arms full of packs of margarine, two of which were given to the fireman. The booty was stowed away in the grub box. Warnings of dire consequences were delivered to the young fireman if a word was uttered about the incident. Absolutely 'scared stiff' of what his parents would say if the 'Special' margarine was taken home, he cobbed them both in the firebox whilst no one was looking. During hard times after the war, coal was in short supply. There was however a very good supply at the shed. Often the thought of a nice blazing fire in the grate at home was simply too much of a temptation. One night after signing off duty, an elderly, very overweight driver loaded his pockets with a few nice slabs of best Yorkshire steam coal. Arriving at the bus stop, he sat down on a convenient garden wall and awaited his bus home. The bus duly arrived and dropped off one passenger. He was so overburdened by his illicit cargo that he couldn't get up quickly enough and the bus left without him. He was therefore forced to abandon some of the booty into the gutter. Another man, faced without fire at home decided to cart some coal to the house where he lived with his elderly mother. Even though it was night-time, his mum spotted him. A strict salvationist, she marched him straight back to the shed and made him put it back with veiled threats of calling the police if he ever did it again. Next, we return for the last time in this chapter to the theme of returning specials from Blackpool. Very late at night, one such special operated by Bolton men would complete its return journey at Horwich carriage sidings. The year is now not entirely certain but in any case falls into the time span covered by this volume very well, the nineteen-fifties. Evening excursions to Blackpool were very popu-

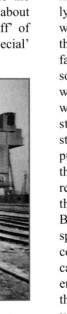

Another view of the concrete store containing just about everything one could need on a footplate. Stanier Crab **42983** looks forlorn amidst a light snowfall.   *S A Leyland*

During that wonderful summer of 1959, I was marked in the disposal link with Tommy Jordan. The job was always made much easier when good quality fire irons were to hand. When you came by tackle that was in good condition you did your best to keep hold of it. For some considerable time I kept my prized possessions under stored engines over on the coal stack road near to Back Crescent Road. Eventually, someone 'removed' them for their own use. This 'Austin' last ran in the early part of 1959 when the metal melted in the big ends whilst Jack Swarbrick and I worked on her on a Horwich to Ashton Moss. In a dreadful state, on February 18th 1961, **49662** has been out of service for almost two years. Final cutting up for scrap at Central Wagon Co; Ince, did not take place until around April of 1962.

lar. Dancing to the strains of Reg Dixon's Wurlitzer in the Tower Ballroom often figured as part of the entertainment. These late returning 'specials' were often dubbed 'The Dancer'. A returning train comprising nine non-corridor coaches had left Preston without incident and was ready to leave the now closed and demolished station at Farington. The site of the station was not very far from Lostock Hall shed. Having got the 'rightaway' from the guard, the driver noted that the vacuum gauge was 'down', indicating that perhaps the communication cord had been pulled. Checking along the train revealed just that. In addition, the door on the offside of the compartment was open. Quite often, to avoid payment of a fare, occupants would make a getaway via this route and leave the station undetected. Was that what had happened? We must wait and see. The journey continued uneventfully. After the last of the passengers had been dropped off at Adlington, the empty carriages were taken on to Horwich carriage sidings. From there, the engine ran light to Bolton shed and its crew signed off duty. Around 3.00am, loud banging on his front door awakened the driver. It was the police requesting his presence at the police station in connection with a murder investigation. The drama now began to unfold. At dead of night, a passed cleaner had dragged himself into the drivers lobby at Lostock Hall shed. He was in an awful state. As well as other serious injuries he

had a badly broken leg. The young man's story was that he and his friend had been attacked in the compartment by a gang and had been badly beaten. The gang then threw both of them out on to the track near to the junction. A search of the line was organized and his friend was found lying on the track. He had sustained very serious injuries and was found to be dead. The one now left alive had dragged and crawled all the way along the metals to the nearby shed to raise the alarm and to ask for assistance. The incident now became a murder inquiry. The carriage in which the two young men had travelled was uncoupled from the rest of the train and put aside with a 24-hour police guard. The vehicle was covered with fine white powder and minutely examined for fingerprints. All to no avail. A week or so dragged by with little to show for the detective's efforts. Then, there came a breakthrough. Doubtless, under cross-examination, the cleaner told the true version of events. Both of them had been out of their compartment on the running boards, peeping into other compartments. Approaching Farington Junction as they attempted to get back to their own compartment they had been swept off by the passage of a train travelling in the opposite direction. One of the two had survived; the other had been less fortunate paying the price for his daring. This chapter could not be concluded without another visit to a favourite route, the Calder

Valley line. For a number of years, at Bolton shed, we had a late Sunday night working for which we signed on at 11/03pm. It gained for itself the nickname of 'The Terror By Night Turn'. Having signed on at the appointed time, we walked to Bolton station to relieve Bank Hall men on a 'Black Five' with a passenger train for York. Servicemen often used this train to return to their barracks, such as Catterick. Starting from Liverpool Exchange, the train called at Wigan, Bolton, Rochdale, Sowerby Bridge and Wakefield where Bolton men relinquished control. Next, a coal train, Calder Bridge to Burnden was operated with a mucky Austerity to contend with. At Bolton, there was much discontent with the working since it went down against the mens name as having worked a Sunday turn even though only a total of 57 minutes were at Sunday rate. On the opposite side of the coin, men who operated a short rest duty to say, Morecambe, would have a total of twenty-eight hours to their name but still only one Sunday debited to them. Often, no one wanted to work the 'Terror By Night' and no wonder. Very early one morning, around 2.00am, the return part of the working with its heavy coal train was halted on the main line approaching Mytholmroyd. Eventually the signal admitting them to the long loop there cleared and they set off. There they had to wait for around twenty to thirty minutes before they could be dealt with. However, what no one knew was that the rearmost six or seven wagons plus brake van had become detached. Before anything wrong was detected a fully fitted newspaper train ran into the stricken vehicles causing terrific damage. A search was made for the guard amongst the wreckage and some time later he was found badly injured. He was taken to hospital but so bad was his condition he never recovered. At the resultant inquiry, it was predicted that the driver, well known for his rough handling of freight trains would be "for it". He refused though to be browbeaten. He was asked at the hearing why his fireman had not exchanged lights with the guard on re-

starting the train. He said that his fireman had attempted to do so. There was no return light from the guard. The driver had then given a short "pop" whistle to draw the attention of the guard but still no reply. The line features such as curvature, embankment and length of train made it difficult to see the brake van. "Why then" asked the questioner had he not sent his fireman back? Had he not read the rule-book? Whereupon the driver answered, "Yes, have you? The driver was now on top and insisted on a rulebook being produced. The questioner was then requested to read out the relevant rule and show where anything was written about proce-

dures if lights were not exchanged. Sure enough, the rule ended after the driver's responsibility with the sounding of the short "pop" whistle. The driver was therefore completely exonerated.

(Below) A pair of 'Black Fives' are seen passing immediately to the north of Farington Curve Junction signal box on Wednesday, June 26th 1963. On the left, and Up line, is (light engine) **45012** (12B -Carlisle Upperby), awaiting clearance to gain access to Farington Curve and subsequently the East Lancashire side of Preston station during a manouvre to 'turn' the engine. Blackpool Central's **45201** (24E) approaches on a Manchester Victoria to Blackpool Central working. *F Dean*

CHAPTER TEN

NEW LAMPS FOR OLD

(Right) Between 1951 and 1957 this Belpaire boilered radial tank wandered from Bolton to Rose Grove, back again to Bolton, then off to Bury before returning to 26C in September of 1956. **50887**, which was 'motor' fitted was sent to Horwich works in December of 1957 where it was eventually cut up. The date of this scene is March 22nd 1953. *M J Blackburn*

At various times throughout the history of the railways there had been economy drives of one kind or another. Concentrating on the time more in keeping with the years akin to those I spent on the railway an early one concerned the introduction of the British Railways 'Standard' types of locomotive. The oiling, or over oiling, according to some drivers, of engines, was a favourite pastime of many. There were various names for oilcans. Some, dating back to the years of the London North Western Railway called them tallow pots. Very early on, axle boxes were filled with melted tallow, which would soften when an axle box became warm. It is more than an even bet that a good deal of this tallow found its way to lots of homes and into domestic chip pans. At that time, lard was very scarce and some of the 'old hands' swore that chips tasted much better when fried in it. That is hardly surprising as it is made from animal fat. When chatting to some of those 'old hands', I have often heard them refer to those wagons using that form of lubrication as 'fat boxers'. They also made the point that trains made up of those wagons took more pulling than later wagons, which depended on the thinner lubricating oil. On shutting off steam, the 'fat boxers' never ran as far as the lubricating oil wagons. On the Lancashire & Yorkshire Railway besides the ordinary oil cans, which we knew more familiarly as 'axle cans' there were a few oil 'feeders'. These 'feeders' were, I suppose, a couple of feet or so in length. They were made from the same tinned sheet material as the oilcans. At the filling end, they would measure about three inches across. A screwed brass stopper secured to the 'feeder' by a small chain facilitated filling of the implement with oil. From the filler end, the 'feeder' tapered to where the oil appeared from an aperture at the opposite extremity. Depressing a small brass nipple discharged the oil, enabling the device to be used to reach the oiling points on inside valve gears from the footplating around the boiler, a much cleaner method of oiling than climbing into the motion-work from beneath whilst the engine stood over a pit. When the BR Standard locomotives began to appear, most of the oiling was done on the outside and there were only five corked oiling points on each side of the engine. The other joints were supplied with grease nipples. The only points underneath the loco which required oiling, were the bogie axles. As designed, those engines were provided with an oil 'bottle' made from tin plate and which had a short spout.

An import to Bolton from Goole, **40685** was a Bolton engine from January 19th 1952 until it left to make Nottingham its home on October 8th 1955. The most these 'Gallopers', as we called them, could hope for was pottering about on Bolton to Liverpool stopping trains with three or four coaches in tow. As they made their way about their haunts, their arrival always seemed to be announced by a clanking of coupling rods, a noise which I always felt was unique to them alone. *M J Blackburn*

Since 1938, Bolton had an allocation of these very strong and useful 0-8-0s until their eventual removal around 1960 when they were concentrated on Newton Heath and Agecroft. If only they had been better designed and given more robust axle boxes and better springing, they might just have survived a little longer. A special favourite of mine seen here at Bolton shed was **49544**. On November 12th 1956, this was the loco on my first firing turn when I was aged just sixteen. *R Panting*

Hey presto, no axle can needed. After a short while, officialdom must have got their heads together. They rather liked the idea of just supplying an oil bottle with spout. That would save the thousands of pounds they were spending on supplying feeders and axle cans. It was now decided that there would be no need for other items, just the bottle. Eventually, memos were circulated to Motive Power Depots to the effect that all items for oiling other than the bottles were to be rounded up, flattened and sent for scrap. There was pandemonium. All the old hands had lost their favourite toy. A few were excepted as they kept their treasures hidden away. Great delight was indulged in when 'lending' them out to fellow sufferers. There are a few known personally to me who would have clapped their hands in glee. Their motto would have been, no oil cans – no oiling. Eventually, those in high office relented, saw the mistake and gave orders for the equipment to be re-instated. Imagine the cost! Fire irons were always in short supply. Clinker shovels soon became dog-eared and although beaten back into shape often were discarded. During 1959, as a member of the disposal link, I very soon became aware of how valuable a long 'Lanky' pricker was. With their tapered end they were a great help in shifting clinker from the far end of a firebox. Next, a good bent dart for moving days of clinker from under the door and a decent clinker shovel and you were set up. For a number of weeks I hid my prized items under stored, condemned engines over on number 14 road. Eventually, someone plundered them and I had to

make do as best I could with what tackle was on the ash pit. Moving on toward the end of steam, which, as we all know was August of 1968, the shortage of parts became acute. A relatively minor defect and an engine might be sidelined for good. A major source of irritation was baffle plates. These were an important piece of equipment. Situated in the firehole their function was to deflect the flow of air down toward the firebed in order to mix it thoroughly with the hot gasses and flames. Often, after a locomotives periodic washout, a new baffle plate would be fitted. Frequently the wrong one would be supplied, usually because there were none of the correct shape and size. The nearest size was therefore fitted. When preparing to take such a loco off shed with an ill fitting baffle plate there would be a frantic search for an old bolt which would be inserted between the appendage and the firehole, just so you could actually get some coal on without too much manoevering. Of course, if the bolt was a bit on the large side, when you pulled the doors together after firing you ran the risk of them jamming. Getting them released was sometimes a nightmare. Even firehole lap plates were missing. Often tempers were frayed between driver and Running Shift Foreman and threats exchanged with the driver refusing to take the engine off shed incomplete. With only a few weeks to go to the complete withdrawal of steam from British Rail, a couple of men, a driver and his fireman were attempting to prepare their Black Five for a freight from Bolton via the Calder Valley line to Healey Mills. Around the middle of the day it was a

fairly pleasant out and back trip. After a while, the fireman reported to his driver that he had been on every engine in the shed and couldn't find any headlamps. He was also without coal pick. Leaving his oiling work, the driver went to speak to the Running Shift Foreman to let him know of the situation. Now it appears that on that morning, both men had got out of their beds on the wrong side and a heated argument took place. The driver for his part stated that they wouldn't be moving until the right equipment was provided. The foreman of course said they could wait there all day if they wanted, as he couldn't care less! Stalemate! The driver swung on his heel and without further ado walked back to his engine where his fireman was waiting, and hauled himself up the three or four steps. Next, he took a book from his jacket pocket, sat himself down, and waited. There the two of them sat. Quite some time had elapsed when, returning from his lunch break, the shed superintendent, Mr. Axford, arrived on the scene. Control had been on the phone as the departure time from Rose Hill sidings had long since passed. Quietly, the official asked what the problem was. The story was told. *'Wilt follow me over to 'trt' store room?'* asked the official, at the same time producing a set of keys. Not knowing the reason for the request, the driver complied with his superior's wishes and followed. One of the keys was inserted into the lock, and the door opened. A flick of the switch brought the light into play and revealed an Aladdin's cave. There, in that concrete building there was just about a gross of everything needed. Headlamps, gauge lamps, firing shovels, coal hammers, the lot. All were brand new. The driver was almost speechless. Why though was the tackle not being issued? Quite simply, if it had been, all of it would have disappeared within a few days. The driver was told to take what he wanted, but not to breathe a word of it to

Until September 1962, Bolton always had an allocation of 3F 0-6-0s, the ex L&Y 'A' classes. One of them was **52345**. This loco, depicted under the coal hopper at Bolton, had been at Crewe works as a shunt engine. During August of 1958 the engine was on the receiving end of a General overhaul at Horwich. Twelve months later it found its way back to Bolton whilst still in good mechanical order. We had three good years out of her before the end came on September 22nd 1962. *J Houghton*

anyone else. In the coming weeks that were left for steam, he was never short of tackle again. He simply requested the keys to the storeroom. All of that which remained was probably bulldozed along with the building itself. Before the end of steam, for a full twelve months, I had formed a hankering to have a job which came with a company car. It is hard to believe that I would have gone down that path had steam operation been allowed to continue. There were not too many of us that hated steam. But the way the steam engine was treated in the final three or four years was an outrage with engines as little as eight years old going to the scrap heap. During that period of time, many locos were rusting hulks often performing miracles. Such was the tolerance of the steam engine. There were of course those Black Fives and Stanier Class 8Fs, which had received heavy repairs as late as 1966. Even one of our BR Standard Class 5MT 4-6-0s No.73069 departed during July of that year for Crewe works with less than two years to go at Bolton before the end of steam. I had many a good run along the Calder Valley main line with that engine on the 10.18pm Bolton to Healey Mills freight. Our return work was Healey Mills to Burnden (Bolton). Many of those units

had been kept in store after the visit to factory, ready to bring out when run down locos were withdrawn. As I write this, I have been able to obtain copies of engine record cards from The National Railway Museum at York. From those cards I note that the envisaged year of final withdrawal for instance, of the Ivatt 2-6-0s numbered 43000-43161 was 1988. A full twenty years after the diesels and electrics took over the running of our railway. It is now a part of history that the enforced withdrawal of steam from our railways was complete by August 4th 1968. Thus,

the motive power that saw us through the industrial revolution was gone for ever as the mainstay of our railways.

(Below) The ash lifting plant and water storage tank are easily visible in this view taken on Bolton shed on March 11th 1961. Having been at Sutton Oak for almost twelve months. 'A' class 0-6-0 No. **52393** arrived at Bolton shed on January 18th 1958. Here, pottering about the shed yard it has three or so months before withdrawal on June 3rd 1961.
J Houghton

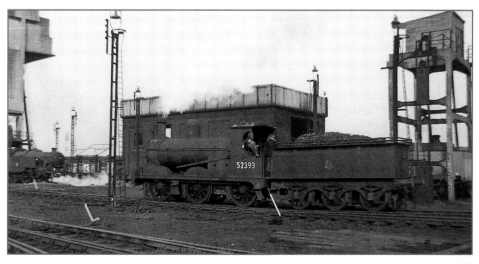

The superheated 'A' Class was the more powerful sister to the saturated 'A' class. With a tractive effort of 27,405lbs, and a cylinder diameter half an inch greater than the Hughes 'Crab' 2-6-0's, they must have been capable of shifting very heavy loads. The one illustrated here was actually a superheated rebuild of the less powerful saturated 'A' classes dating back to 1913. A July 1953 transfer to Bolton from Sowerby Bridge shed, **52575** is out of use in August of 1955 at Crescent Road shed. When I made my first visit to Horwich works in March 1956 the boiler from this loco was lying in the snow near to the scrap line. Still in place on the smokebox was its 26C shed plate.
Brian Morrison

(**Below**) This 'A' class had originally been one of the superheated variety but with a round-topped firebox and extended smoke box. Later in their lives, engines so built had their super-heater boilers and extended smoke boxes removed, thus becoming saturated steam locos. Engines thus dealt with like **52523** illustrated here were always identified by the retained, longer sandboxes. The location is Radcliffe West Junction and the 0-6-0 is operating an enthusiast's special on July 28th 1962 with less than one month to go before withdrawal along with 52345 as the last of Bolton's 'A' classes. As 1Z30, the special at this stage was en-route to Radcliffe South Junction and the electrified line to Manchester Victoria after having travelled from Bury Bolton Street via Radcliffe North Junction and the west fork to reverse at Bradley Fold. On the left (above the leading coach) is the Radcliffe sub-station and battery house for the 'electric' line. In the centre (level with the signal box gable end) are the two large goods sheds in Radcliffe Goods Yard on Spring Lane together with the elevated profile of Spring Lane Brewery. In days gone by, Canal Siding was located behind the West box whilst Whittaker Street Siding ran parallel with and to the right of the telegraph poles to the right of the picture. On the skyline to the extreme right is the is Stand Church, Whitefield. *E F Bentley*

(Above) No. **51519** rests between duties at it's home shed, 26C. The engine still carries the Ramsbottom type of safety valve and due to lack of vacuum pipes must have been of the pure steam brake variety. We saw the last of these efficient and popular little locomotives at Bolton in November of 1961 when 51408 departed for Agecroft. *Frank Dean*

(Below) When this pleasing view was taken, saddle tank No. **51371** was allocated to Newton Heath shed. It must therefore have been borrowed by Bolton in order to fulfill its requirements for power. At Haslams sidings in most unkempt condition, the loco is ready with the afternoon trip to Bullfield. There is a pause in operations whilst the guard and driver converse. The 0-6-0 is another of the steam brake variety. The date here is 27/7/60. *Authors collection*

(Above) Two Bolton engines coupled together bunker-to-bunker form an intriguing picture on March 7th 1964. The two locos are moving what is likely to be a transfer trip from Haslams Sidings to Bullfield. The engines are ex-LMS 0-6-0 standard side tank shunting engine No. **47520** in front, whilst the train engine is BR Standard Class 2MT 2-6-2 tank No. **84013**. Just why double heading was resorted to is unclear since the train is not a lengthy one. *R Farrell*

(Centre) Just why there was a need for Bolton to exchange its last ex-L&Y saddle tank No. 51408 for Agecroft's 0-6-0 Dock tank, No. **47165** shown here, I really do not know. That exchange took place on 18th November 1961. Halliwell goods yard and its power station in the right background had been well served by the L&Y machine for years. The date of this homely little scene is September 14th 1963. *D Hampson*

(Right) Strictly speaking, this ex-L&Y saddle tank has no part in this book, for it is not a Bolton engine, it is just simply pausing on 9K, *en route* from Parsonage Colliery to Yates Duxbury's at Bury. Although its smoke box has the number 51456, it never did carry the BR number having been sold to an outside contractor during LMS days. The engine is now preserved on the Keighley & Worth Valley line. *V A Sidlow*

(Right) Waiting for the road at the shed outlet at Bolton MPD is 'A' class **52345**. The 0-6-0 is ready for a spell of pilot duties around Bullfield, Haslams and Burnden sidings. Later in the day it will bring loco coal on to the shed. The date is May 25th 1960. *J Houghton*

(Centre) A once familiar footplate view on 'A' Class No. 52345. To the right the round aperture with window is the cylinder lubricator. The two large valve handles control the injector steam valves, whilst the two boiler water gauge glasses with their protectors figure prominently. The blower valve is visible immediately over the residing brew can.
J Houghton

(Below) Just before the Christmas of 1957, Bolton received two of the roughest 'Austin Sevens' you could possibly imagine, 49618 and 49662 from Lees (Oldham) shed. The former, the worst of the two, was in the 'shops' at Horwich early in 1958 receiving a General overhaul. She was one of the few of her class to have the then new BR crest applied to the tender. Sadly, in this view taken on April 2nd 1960 she is becoming badly run down again. In January of 1960 the final nine or ten survivors were concentrated on Newton Heath and Agecroft sheds to wear themselves out, pottering about from yard to yard like this one. Withdrawal for **49618** came in October 1961. *Frank Dean*

(Above) Bolton's 'Big Tank' No. **42656** was supplied new to the depot on February 3rd 1941 and spent the greater part of its life at Crescent Road. I always remember her as being a very economical engine on both coal and water and never struggling for steam. Here, the 2-6-4 tank is operating the 3/20pm Blackpool Central to Manchester train passing Lytham St Annes Golf Club; fireman Bernard Bentley is visible via cab side window on September 9th 1962.
Frank Dean

(Centre) During 1940, **42653** was the only Stanier tank to be produced at Derby works. It was allocated from new to Bolton where it stayed all its life of just under twenty-two years when withdrawal came in September 1962. Here the loco is resting at its home depot during July of 1960. *J Houghton*

(Below) Another view of **42656**, this time doing a shunt. Smoke from the Austerity (90466), which was in process of raising steam, had been a problem and complaints were being received from local residents. On this occasion, it was decided to push the Austerity into the shed to disperse the smoke more effectively. The date here is 26th May 1963. *D Hampson*

(Right-top) Running light engine at Farington Curve on the line to Preston, Lostock Hall men are en-route to Blackpool Central to operate the 4/30pm all stations to Bolton with Bolton tank No. **42654**. This loco was a lifelong resident of Bolton shed between April 20th 1941, as a new engine, and withdrawal on 21st November 1964. *Frank Dean*

(Right-centre) On July 11th 1962, Bolton's Stanier tank No. **42630** is operating the 5/47pm from Horwich to Manchester. The train is approaching Moses Gate near to Green Lane Bridge. As was normal at that time, there is a stores van coupled next to the engine. Above the rear coach, the outline of Bolton shed's coal hopper is just about visible through the smoke haze. *D Hampson*

(Bottom of page) Always regarded as a good steamer, **42565** was a July 1947 arrival to 26C from Uttoxeter. Here the engine is operating the 2/30pm from Rochdale to Wigan on Saturday January 20th 1962 having just left Bradley Fold. *E F Bentley*

BOLTON'S CLASS *4* TANK ENGINES

(Right-upper) A 12th February 1966 arrival from Carnforth, **42663** along with 42656 was one of the last two Stanier passenger tanks to leave Bolton shed in December of the same year. Here, the ex-Carnforth loco is pictured at Hindley North on April 16th 1966. The fireman is racing back to the footplate after some duty or other whilst the driver is Bert Welsby.
courtesy H Welsby

(Centre) Fairburn tank No. **42183** arrived at Bolton shed as a transfer from Lees (Oldham) on April 13th 1964. Pictured on November 28th 1965 at Bolton shed, the engine has a little under twelve months before withdrawal from service. *S A Leyland*

(Below) At the time that 42289 was transferred to Bolton in June of 1956, it was the only 'rocker bar' tank engine on Bolton's books. It was often 'steam shy'. Here the Fairburn machine is operating an RCTS rail tour, which included some lines used only for freight. The train has arrived at Halliwell, near Bolton on Saturday April 4th 1959. *B Hilton*

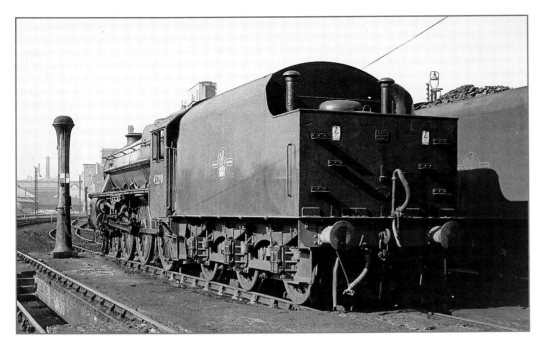

(**Left-upper**) Bolton shed's first Black Five and a special favourite of mine was **45290**. The 4-6-0 arrived from Newton Heath to be allocated to 26C on February 10th 1962. Waiting her next turn of duty at Bolton she looks fine on March 28th 1965. *H L Holland*

(**Left-centre**) When Black Five No. 45110 arrived at Bolton shed as a transfer from Stafford on July 18th 1965, no-one could have guessed what the future held in store for her. To say that her condition was poor is an understatement, she was rough. In this condition, the 4-6-0 ran on until suddenly removed from traffic on April 13th 1966. In the engine status book at Bolton, instead of the blue tick signifying availability, there was a red one, which meant that the engine was awaiting admission to 'factory'. No specific date for her departure to Cowlairs works is known but 45110 had arrived there by April 22nd. The visit was a protracted one of fourteen weeks. The Stanier machine eventually left Cowlairs works around July 15th and had been used at other sheds before arriving back at Bolton MPD at 10/40pm on July 22nd having been collected from Newton Heath depot. A good deal of work had been undertaken with a partial re-paint and a large hole in the smoke box having been rectified. All this meant was that 45110 had been transformed into a very good engine. However, before she could really be put to the test there followed a period of fifteen months in store, kept in reserve until other less serviceable locos were too worn out to be economically repaired. It is now history that 45110 is preserved at the Severn Valley Railway and is named *RAF Biggin Hill*. In this undated view, 45110 has lost her number plates and instead has the figures neatly painted on the smoke box door as she waits on number 12 road at Bolton shed. *H L Holland*

(**Left-lower**) On December 14th 1963 there arrived from Carlisle Kingmoor the worst Black Five I ever worked on. **45351** was always in filthy condition as portrayed here on February 28th 1965. She was not typical of the class as a whole. Neither injector would stay on for long and everything about the loco suggested it was too much effort. No tears were shed when this Black Five was passed on to Lostock Hall on June 26th 1965. *H L Holland*

(Above) Prior to becoming a Bolton engine, Stanier Black Five No. **45377** had been at Bury shed up until the closure of that depot in April 1965. The 4-6-0 rests on number 13 road near to the Crescent Road side of the shed during August 1967.   *H L Holland*

(Centre) This Stanier Black Five had been a Newton Heath loco for some years until transferred to Bury on the 14th of November 1964. With the closure of that latter depot, 45104 moved down the road to Bolton on April 10th 1965, from where it was withdrawn on June 29th 1968 at the end of steam at Bolton. Here, the 4-6-0 is shown inside Bolton shed on number five road on June 1st 1968.
N E Preedy

(Right-lower) Agecroft had been a long-standing home of Black Five No. **44781**. Short spells at Stockport and at Newton Heath followed closure of Agecroft shed and a month or so before closure of 9K this Stanier machine was based at Bolton. A final allocation was to Carnforth on July 1st 1968, but that was not quite the end for 44781. After a short period of storage at Carnforth, the engine was used in a film when a crash was staged at Bartlow in Essex. Kings of Norwich afterwards cut up the engine on site. The date of this scene at Bolton shed is June 16th 1968.
N E Preedy

(Right) Having arrived at Blackpool shed on March 1st 1952, Black Five **44947** stayed there until made surplus to requirements by dieselisation, and of course the closure of Blackpool Central Station in November 1964. Whilst Bolton men operated the 4/35pm Rochdale to Blackpool Central express, I worked on her many times when I was on passenger work. In this undated view, the engine is caught on camera whilst filling up her tender tank from the water crane up the shed yard at Bolton. *Authors collection*

(Centre) Amongst the first allocated Stanier Class 8F's to Bolton shed since LMS days was **48371**. At the time of its arrival, I remember it being said that these 'starred' Class 8's were specifically for a new speeded up freight service into Yorkshire. The other two arrivals were 48495 and 48547, all three being transferred to Bolton shed on June 20th 1964. The date here is 28th February 1965. *H L Holland*

(Below) Bolton Trinity Street on June 10th 1965 with Stanier Class 8F No. **48547** running light engine along the Up Through line. The penultimate loco off Horwich works prior to its closure for steam repairs, the 2-8-0 was transferred to Bolton from Hasland on June 20th 1964, only a couple of months after it's repairs were completed. *H L Holland*

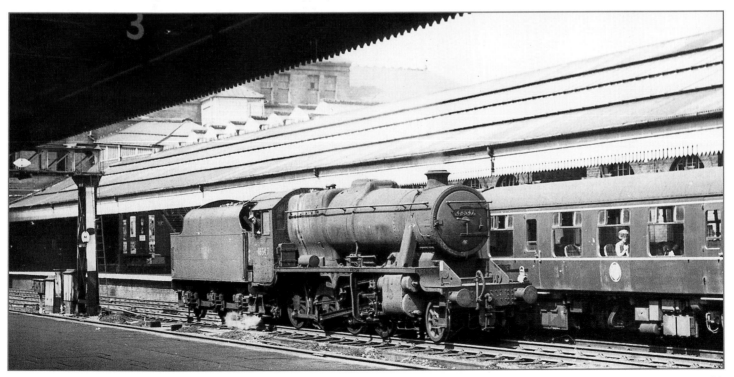

(Right) When steam pressure was allowed to fall too low to enable use to be made of the vacuum system to turn the engine, good old fashioned pushing power had to be resorted to. The man nearer the camera on Bolton shed's turntable is Passed Fireman Neil Grundy whilst the other footplateman is not identified. **48773** arrived from Buxton in the week commencing 19th September 1964. By late April of 1966, the engine had reached a stage of 'shopping' or scrapping. From the 5th May 1966, Bolton had the loco recorded as awaiting a decision and it was shown as out of service at Newton Heath. Usually when a loco was recorded thus it meant permanently. Two determining features were the state of the ash pan and lateral play in the driving wheel axle boxes, causing the driving wheels to rub the frame. By late May the 2-8-0 was accepted by Crewe works for a heavy intermediate overhaul. On returning to Bolton shed on July 1st 1966, the engine was placed in store until April 9th 1967 so our picture is between that date and closure of Bolton shed on 30th June 1968. It is well known that 48773 survives at the Severn Valley Railway.

Bart van der Leew

(Centre) A transfer to Bolton very near to the end for steam, **48720** arrived on May 6th 1968 just about a month before the end of steam at Bolton. In the summer sunshine, at Bolton shed, the Stanier machine looks in fine fettle on June 8th 1968. *N E Preedy*

(Right-lower) Two Bolton engines operating a Labour Party excursion from Westhoughton to Blackpool North. The pilot engine is the green liveried BR Standard Class 5 4-6-0 No.**73014** in charge of driver Bert Welsby. The train engine is Black Five No. **45260** with Frank Rimmer at the controls. The location is the Down Slow line at Standish Junction on June 3rd 1967. The BR Standard was, naturally, a popular loco with the enthusiasts who visited Bolton shed to clean engines. Its green paintwork looked good when given their attention, although all was not well with 73014's boiler and on the 10th of July after operating a Bolton to Bamfurlong working she worked no more. *courtesy Bert Welsby*

(**Right**) Two Class 2 locos, several generations apart and both still working hard for their living. At Bolton shed, coupled bunker to bunker are **84019,** nearest to camera, and **50850,** the last of the ex L&Y radial tanks. Just about the only feature they have in common is the size of the chimney. On 17th September, the day before this scene, 50850 had operated a Central Lancashire Rail Tour, which took in Oldham Road Goods Station, Middleton Junction, Oldham, Rochdale, Bury, Bolton, Lostock Junction and Chorley to Blackburn. Prior to the tour, 50850 had been given some attention at Horwich Works, and must surely have been one of the last L&Y loco to have been so treated there. She worked on at Southport until October of 1961 when she was withdrawn from traffic. By contrast, 84019 found its way to Eastleigh by November of 1965, from where it was withdrawn.
courtesy S Taylor

(**Centre**) Minus its tankside crest, push and pull fitted class 2MT tank No. **84014** pauses at Bolton shed next to an Ivatt 2-6-0 trials loco from Horwich works. This 2-6-2 loco 'lived' a bit longer at Bolton shed than its sister loco No. 84013. It moved from Lees (Oldham) shed to Bolton on February 21st 1959, but was moved to Stockport at the same time as 84013 on December 19th 1964. The date here is June 2nd 1963.   *D Hampson*

(**Below**) After a spell working out of Lees (Oldham) shed, **84013** moved to Bolton on May 2nd 1959. The engine is depicted here at Horwich about to leave with the 4/57pm pull and push service to Blackrod on an un-recorded date. On December 19th 1964, this BR Standard 2-6-2 tank was moved on to Stockport. All traces of this friendly little station have now gone and the area has become parkland.
H L Holland

(Right) Formerly a Crewe South loco, **48559** had a very short 'innings' at Bolton shed from August 12th 1967, until very early in January 1968 when it was withdrawn from traffic. The end came in April 1968 when Drapers of Hull cut her up. The 2-8-0 is shown standing on number 12 road at Bolton shed not long after its arrival. There has been sufficient time for those enthusiasts who frequented Bolton shed to paint on the smoke box 9K, and 'Bolton' on the front buffer beam.

H L Holland

(Below) During February of 1968 a line up of Staniers are placed neatly for the cameraman, just inside Bolton shed. The 2-8-0 nearest the camera, **48111**, blew a cylinder head off on March 6th whilst running light engine to shed just a few days after this view was taken. It was withdrawn from traffic in the week March 16th 1968

P Salveson

(Above) Positioned just right for the fire to be dropped into the sump on the ash pit, **48111** awaits disposal duties in this un-dated scene. Taking up the fire bars, it was possible to push the unwanted fire and clinker into the ash pan. With a long rake, most of that deposited could be pushed through into the pit or the sump. After all that it was suitably quenched with the water spray and lifted in the bucket situated at the bottom of the sump then tipped into waiting wagons. *Authors collection*

(Far left) Formerly a fireman, Bill Buchanan left the footplate and became one of the sheds steamraisers. Here he takes time out to pose for this happy shot. The date is not recorded. *Bart van der Leeuw*

(Left) Bert Welsby is back at the controls of a steam engine. The location is Horwich Works during March or April of 1975. The B1 locomotive *Mayflower*, here numbered **1306**, was given a re-paint in the works. Bert is shown along with the 4-6-0 prior to departing light engine for Manchester where relief was provided. *courtesy Bert Welsby*

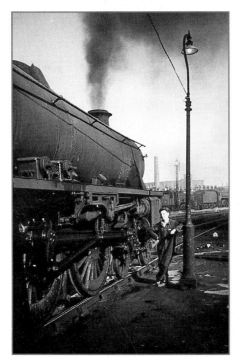